Van Gogh's Sun flowers

Edited by
Jennifer A. Thompson

Essays by
Tara Contractor
Caroline Shields
Jennifer A. Thompson

Philadelphia Museum of Art
Distributed by Yale University Press,
New Haven and London

"I'd like to do a decoration for the stud
The whole thing will therefore be a sy

—Vincent van Gogh to Theo van Gogh
August 21 or 22, 1888

othing but large Sunflowers....
iony in blue and yellow."

Contents

Foreword

By all accounts, the two years Vincent van Gogh spent in the South of France were transformative. He had left the competitive art world of Paris behind in February 1888 to seek inspiration in the sunlight, color, terrain, and people of Provence. His development as an artist during the ensuing months is richly documented not only in his art but also in letters to his brother Theo. In Arles and Saint-Rémy-de-Provence, Van Gogh discovered and made his own the motifs for which he is most celebrated today: Provençal landscapes with tall cypresses or groves of olive trees, sensitive portraits of a postman and his family, and penetrating investigations of irises, oleanders, roses, and sunflowers. This volume is devoted to the flower Van Gogh most identified with and that encapsulates many of his hopes, ambitions, and innovations.

Since 1963, thanks to the generosity of the collectors Carroll Sargent Tyson, Jr., and Helen Roebling Tyson, the Philadelphia Museum of Art has been home to one of five large canvases of sunflowers that Van Gogh painted in Arles. An armful of these blooms—bought from a market or picked from a local garden—led to an exuberant burst of production during a single week in mid-August 1888. As he wrote to Theo on August 21 or 22, "I'm painting with the gusto of a Marseillais eating bouillabaisse, which won't surprise you when it's a question of painting *large* SUNFLOWERS." Five months later he returned to painting sunflowers, more somber and determined to create canvases that could be shown together in novel ways.

As the essays by Jennifer Thompson, Caroline Shields, and Tara Contractor in this publication reveal, Van Gogh's *Sunflowers* reflect his evolving ideas about creativity, decoration, and presentation. The singular subject, returned to repeatedly, became a vehicle for experiments with color, form, and expression. When Paul Gauguin joined Van Gogh in October at the Yellow House, the modest building in Arles that would be their home and studio during a short but eventful interval, still life became a focus of stimulating debates about the roles of close observation and imagination in the creation of works of art. That dialogue, and Van Gogh's persistent drive to say something new in his art, contributed to the attention he devoted to placing the *Sunflowers* within

—Daniel H. Weiss

The George D. Widener Director and Chief Executive Officer

appropriate frames and arranging them in welcoming, consoling, and humane ways.

One of the striking findings that emerges in this volume is Van Gogh's fixation on experiencing the sunflower paintings in ensembles. In the studio and guest bedroom of the Yellow House, in the Paris shop of Julien Tanguy, and in the exhibition rooms of Les Vingt in Brussels, he arranged them in multiples. Today, when the canvases are scattered across five countries on three continents, opportunities to encounter them together are exceedingly rare. The generosity of our colleagues at the National Gallery in London has given Philadelphia audiences just such an opportunity, allowing us to appreciate two of the *Sunflowers* together and to observe how they interact with and play off each other. Regarding a yellow-ground painting from August 1888 alongside a turquoise-ground canvas made in January 1889, one can learn a great deal about the variety of color and feeling conveyed in the artist's brushwork. I thank Jennifer Thompson, the Gisela and Dennis Alter Curator of European Painting, Curator of the John G. Johnson Collection, and Head of European Art at the Philadelphia Museum of Art, for her care and attention in arranging this exceptional exchange and in spearheading this publication.

For making this engaging encounter possible, we owe thanks to the Gloria and Jack Drosdick and the Harriet and Ronald Lassin Funds for Special Exhibitions at the Philadelphia Museum of Art. We are grateful as well for their help in underwriting this publication, which vividly brings to life the textured surfaces and complementary nature of all five sunflower canvases. The paintings' ability to harmonize was one of Van Gogh's guiding principles, as he explained to Theo in that same August letter: "If I carry out this plan there'll be a dozen or so panels. The whole thing will therefore be a symphony in blue and yellow."

The Sunflowers

Vincent van Gogh (Dutch, 1853–1890)

Sunflowers

Arles, August 1888
Oil on canvas
36¼ × 28¾ in. (92 × 73 cm)
The National Gallery, London: Bought, Courtauld Fund, 1924, NG3863

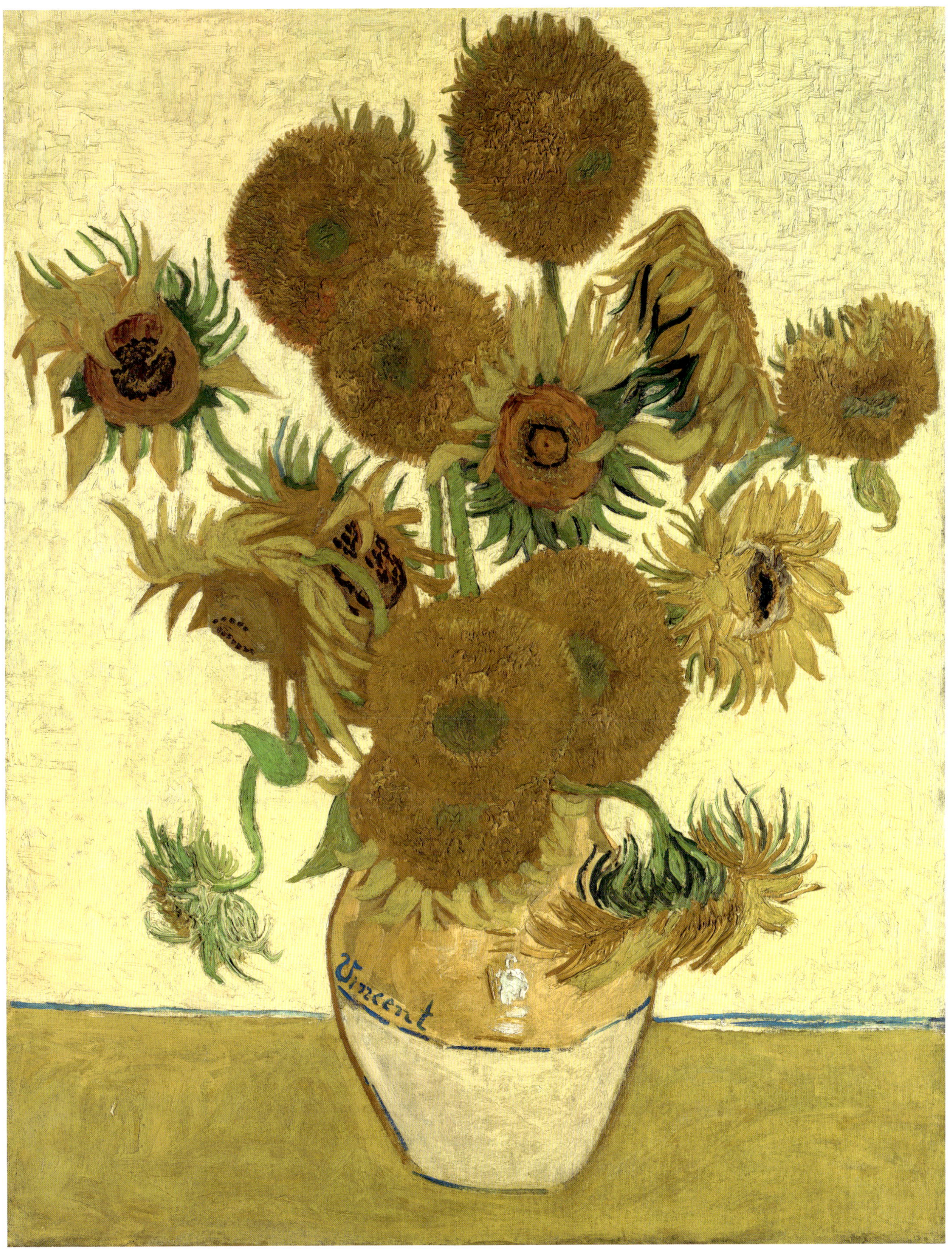
Vincent

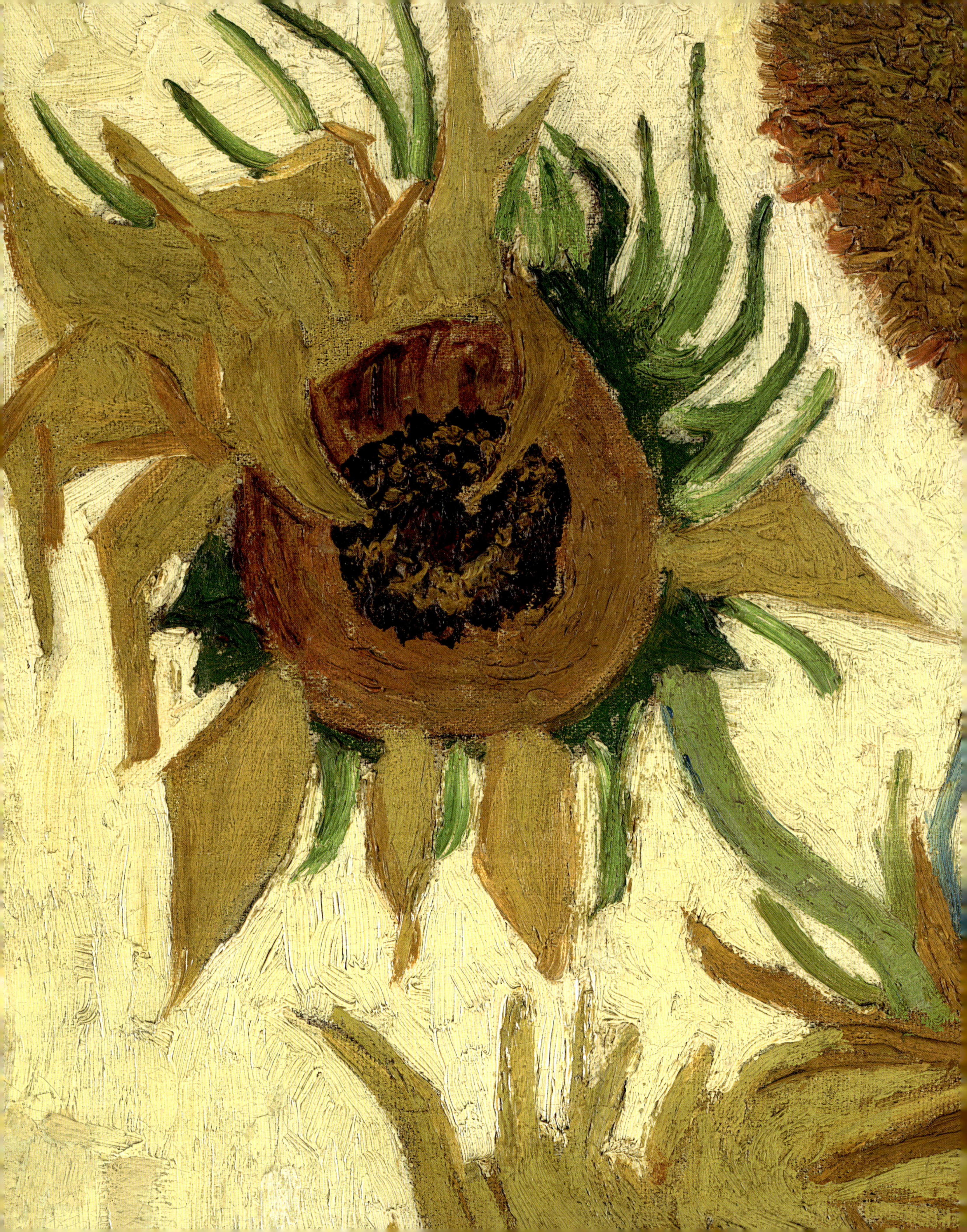

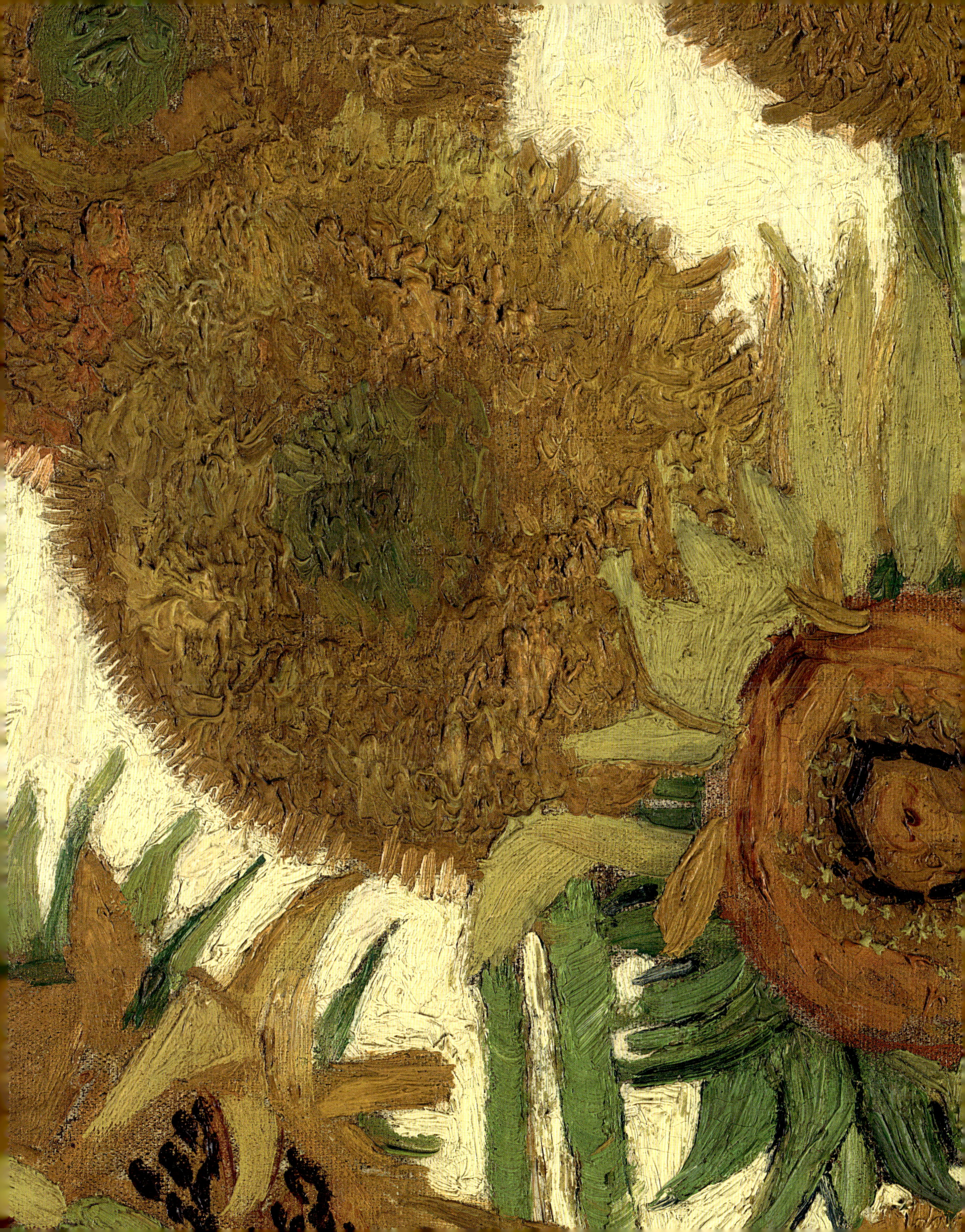

Vincent van Gogh

Sunflowers

Arles, August 1888

Oil on canvas

36¼ × 28¾ in. (92 × 73 cm)

Bayerische Staatsgemäldesammlungen, Neue Pinakothek, Munich, 8672

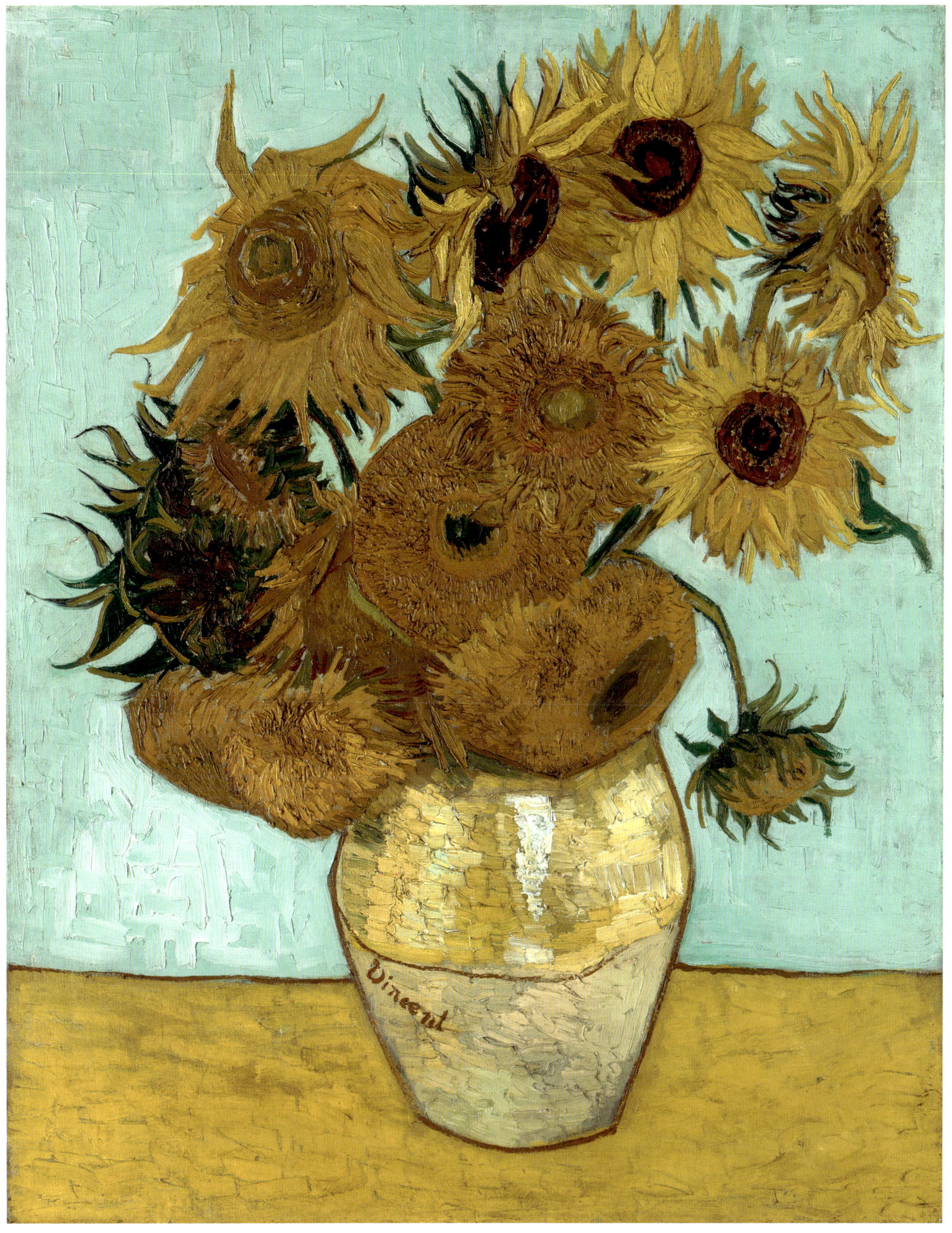
Vincent

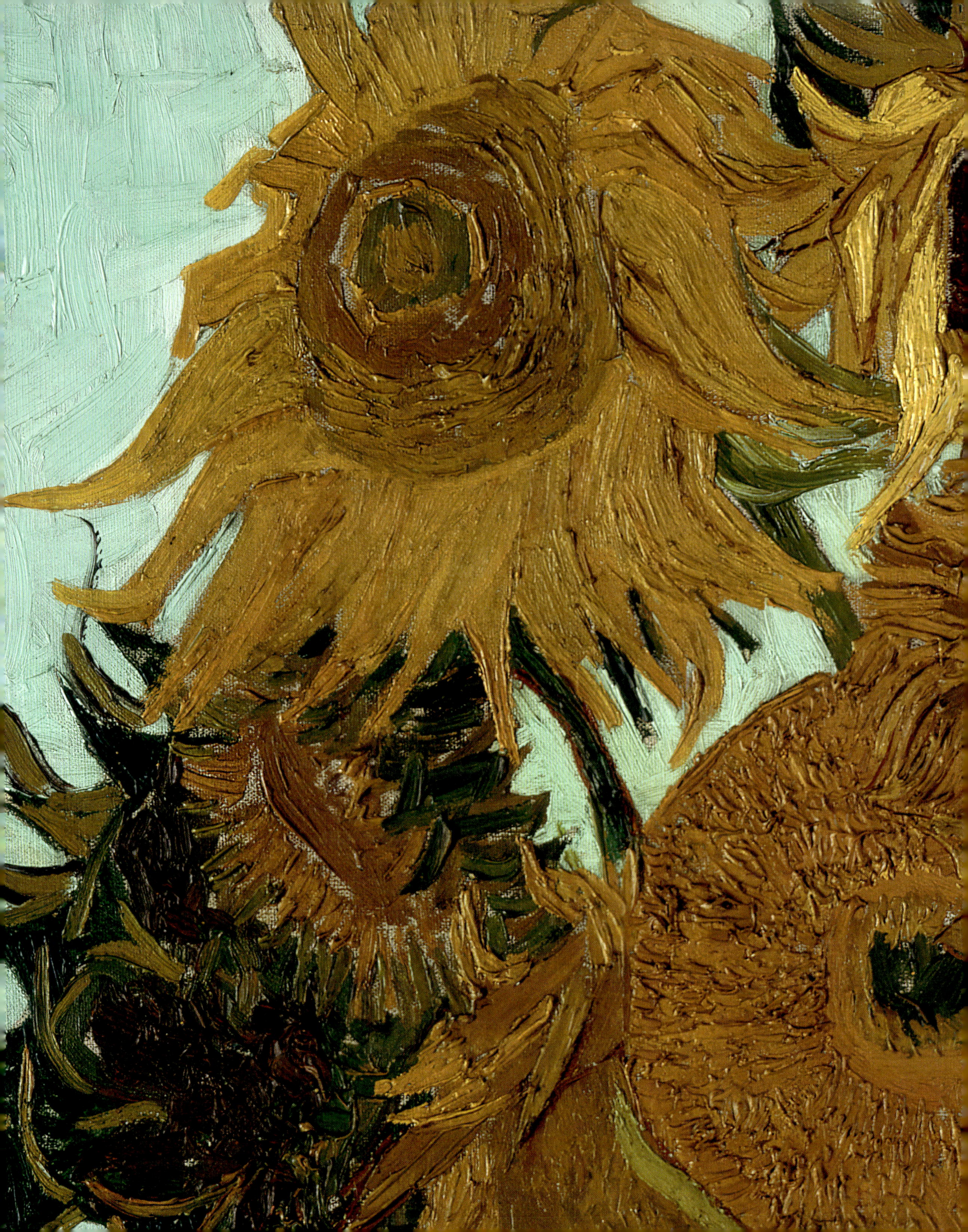

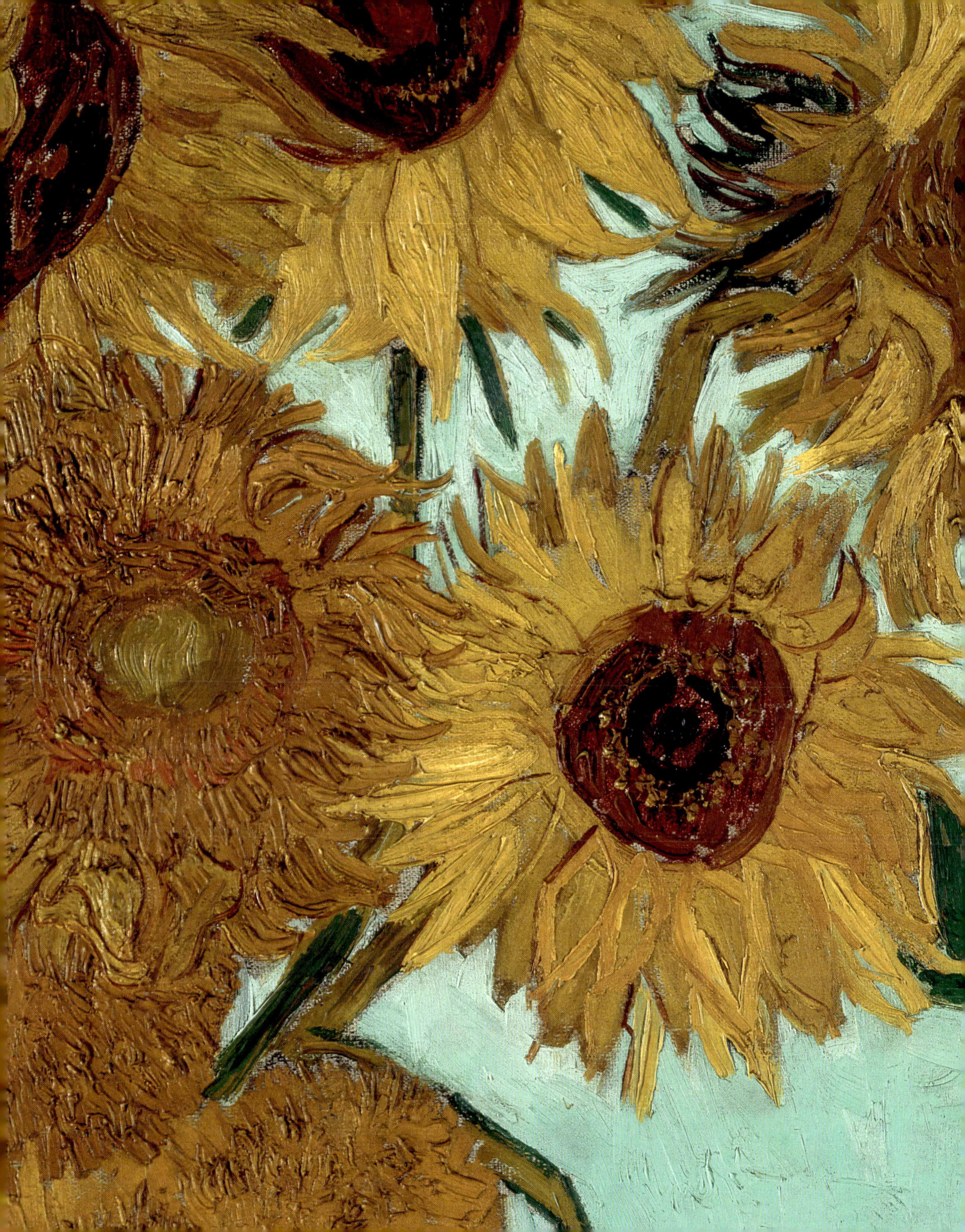

Vincent van Gogh

Sunflowers

Arles, likely December 1888

Oil on canvas

39 9/16 × 30 1/8 in. (100.5 × 76.5 cm)

Sompo Museum of Art, Tokyo

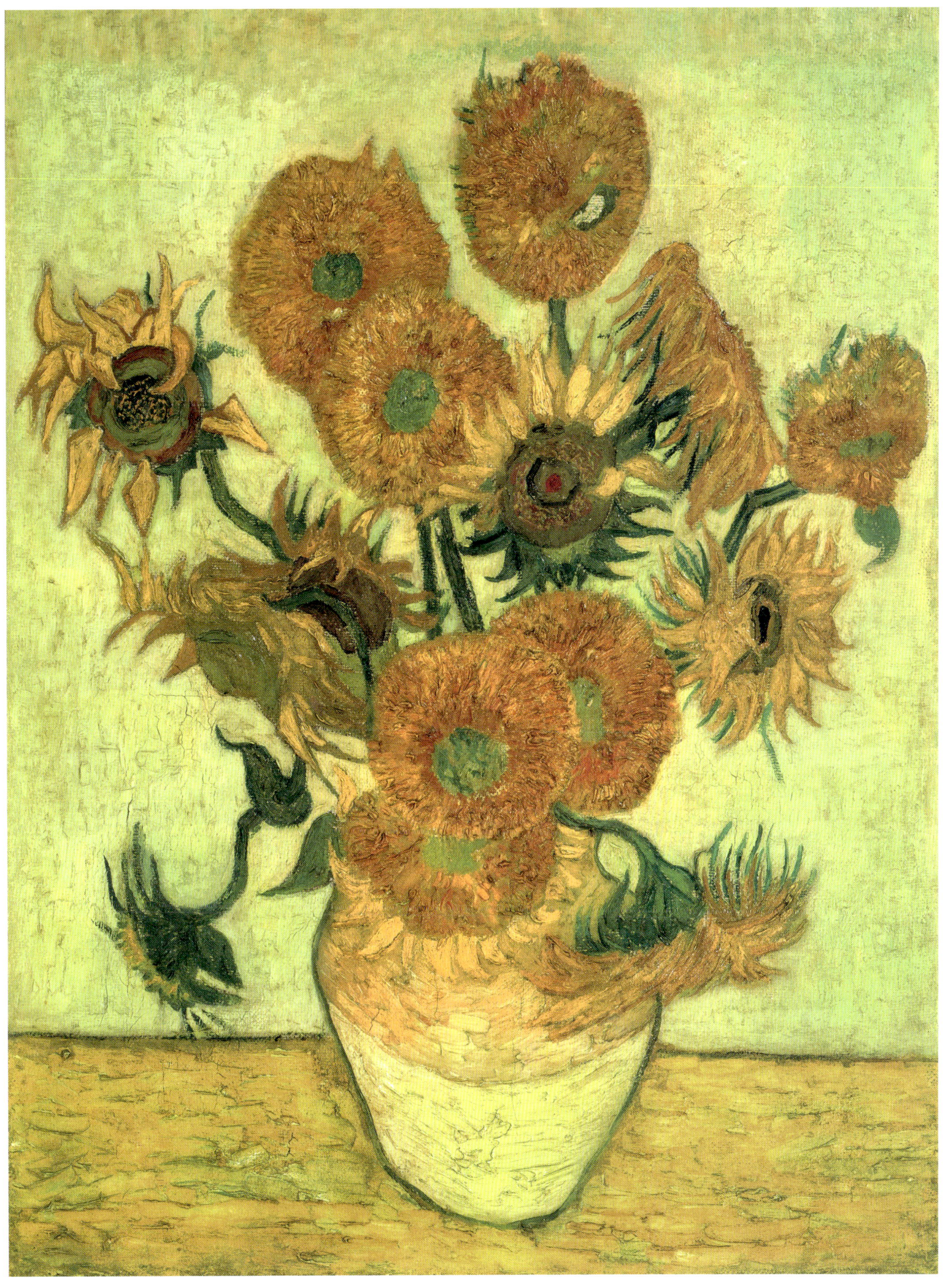

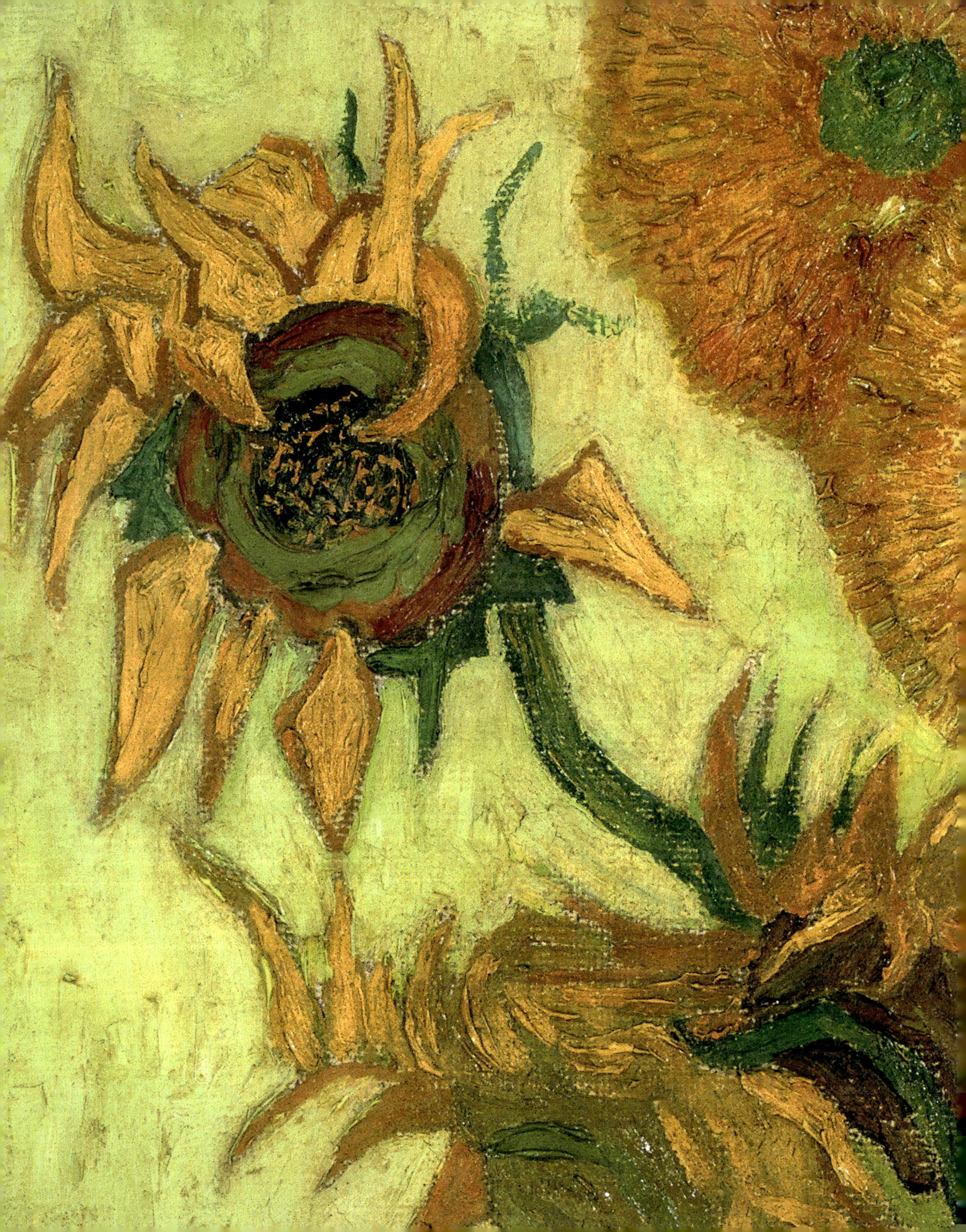

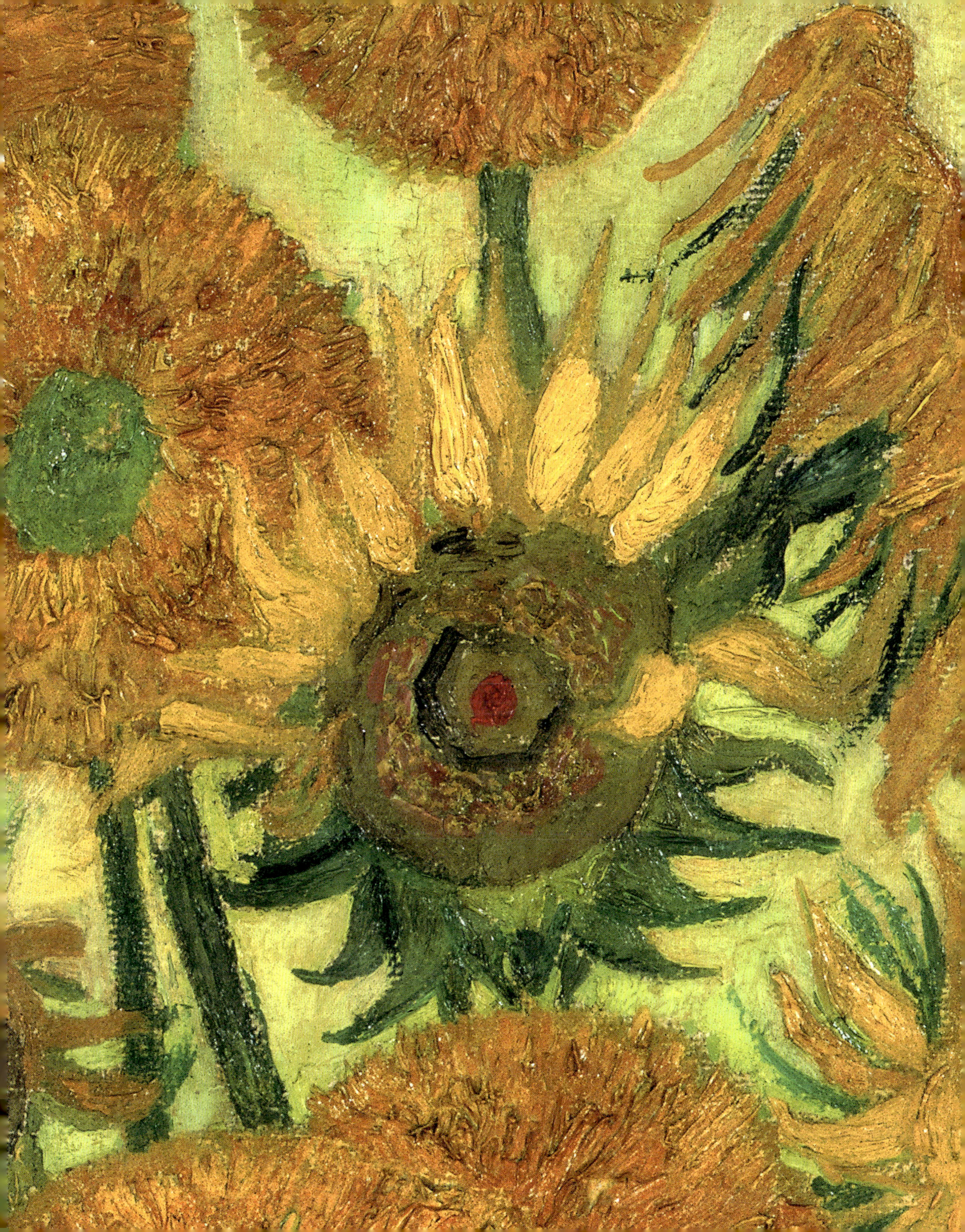

Vincent van Gogh

Sunflowers

Arles, January 1889

Oil on canvas

36⅜ × 28 in. (92.4 × 71.1 cm)

Philadelphia Museum of Art: The Mr. and Mrs. Carroll S. Tyson, Jr., Collection, 1963-116-19

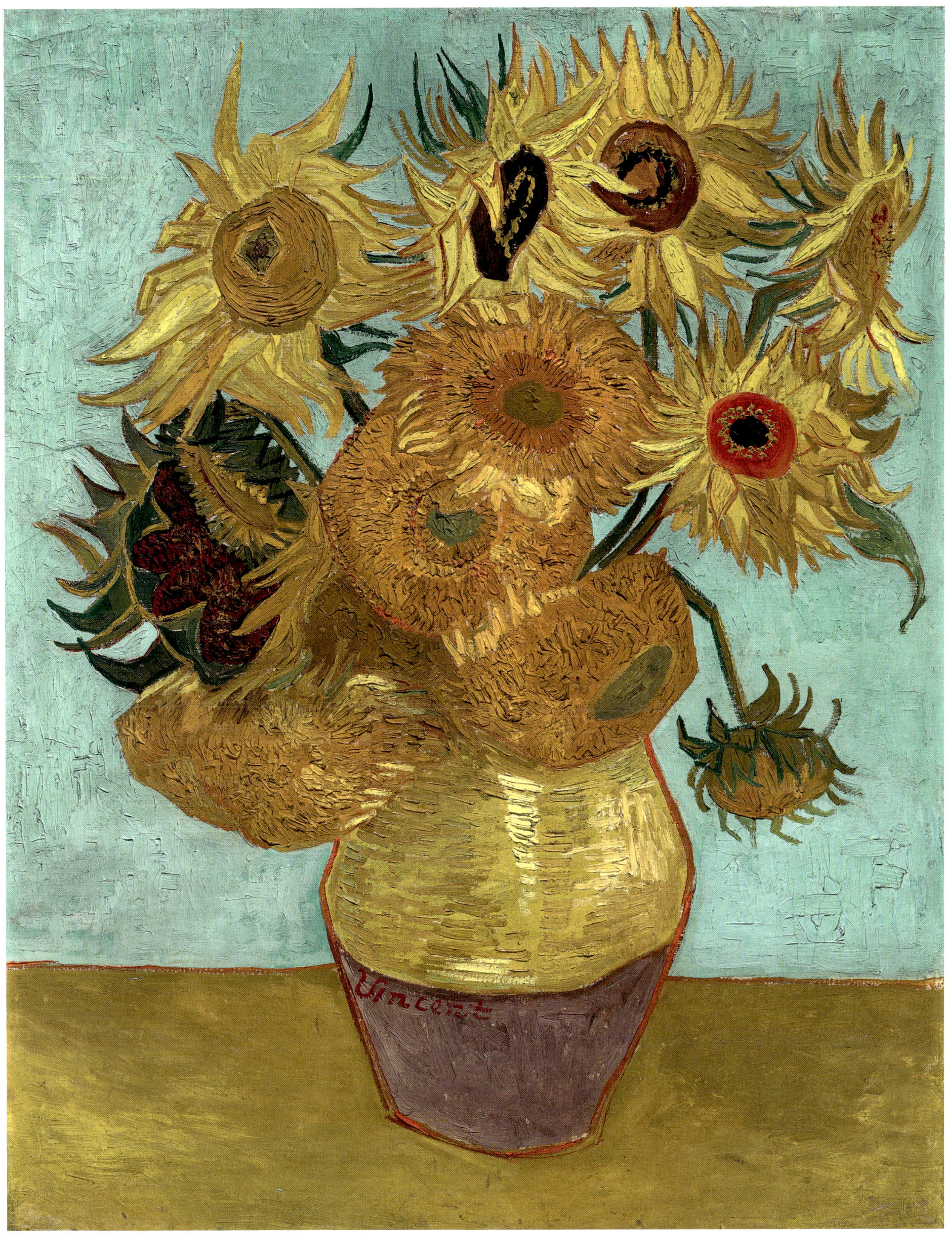
Vincent

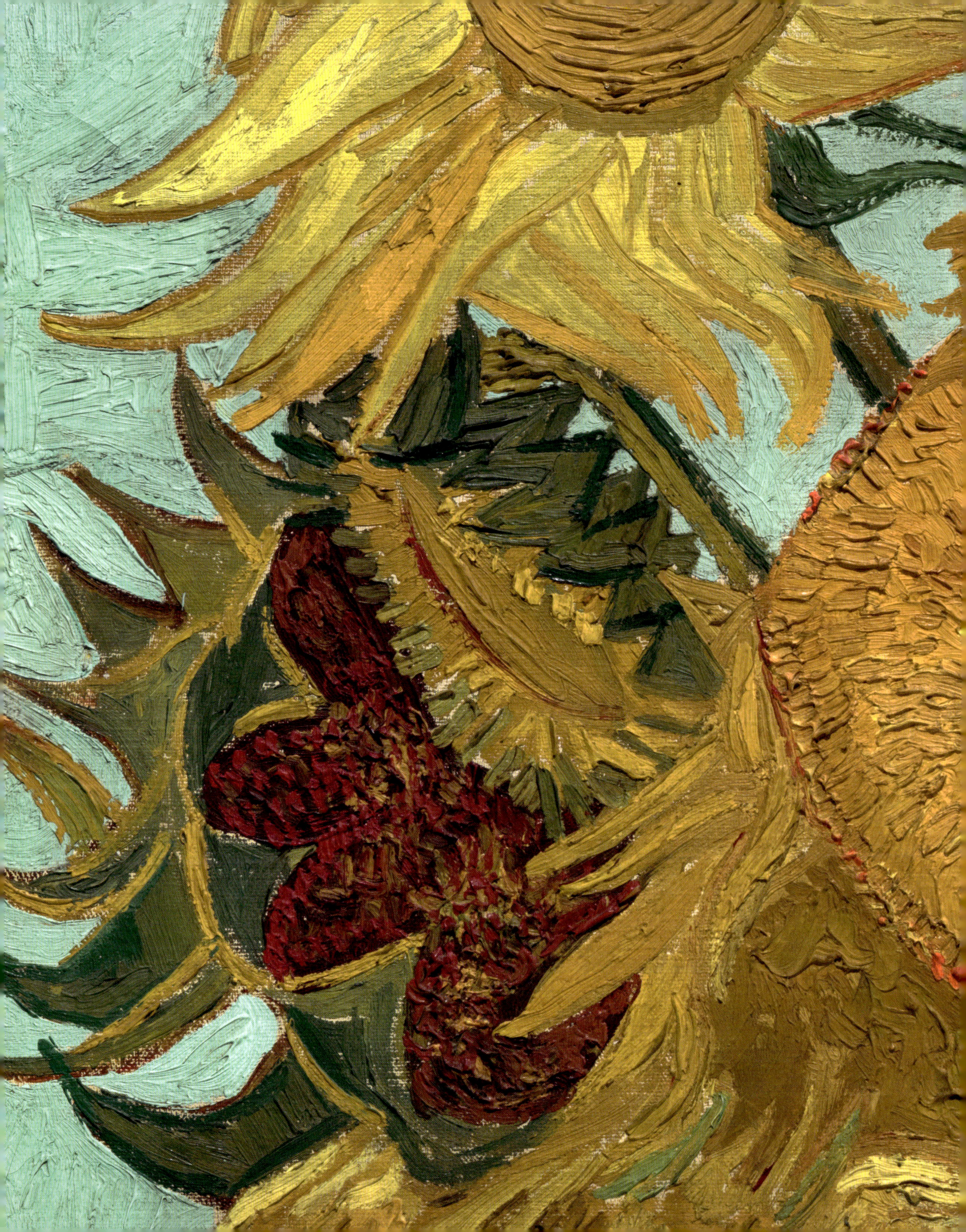

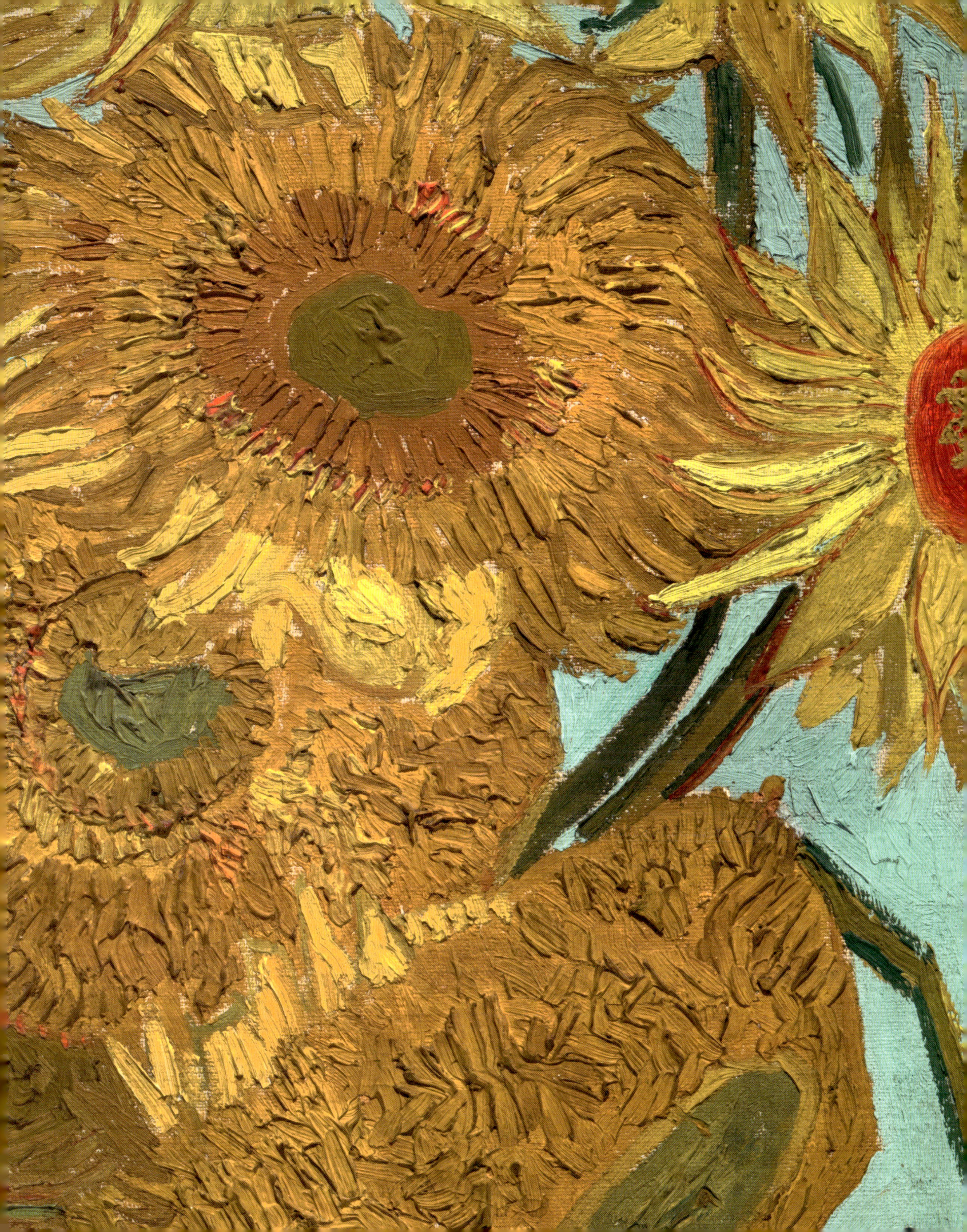

Vincent van Gogh

Sunflowers

Arles, January 1889

Oil on canvas

$37\frac{3}{8} \times 28\frac{3}{4}$ in. (95 × 73 cm)

Van Gogh Museum, Amsterdam (Vincent van Gogh Foundation)

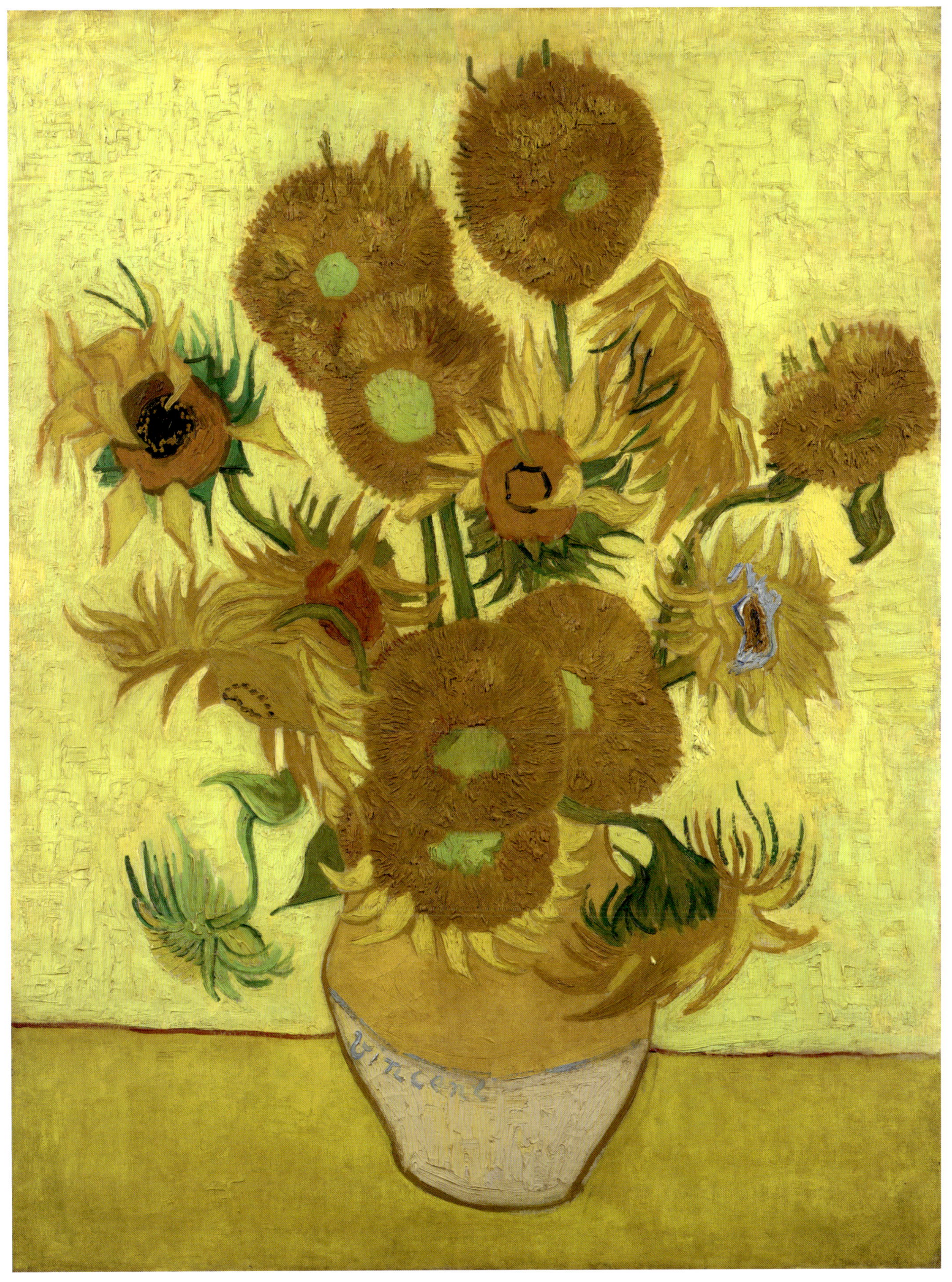
Vincent

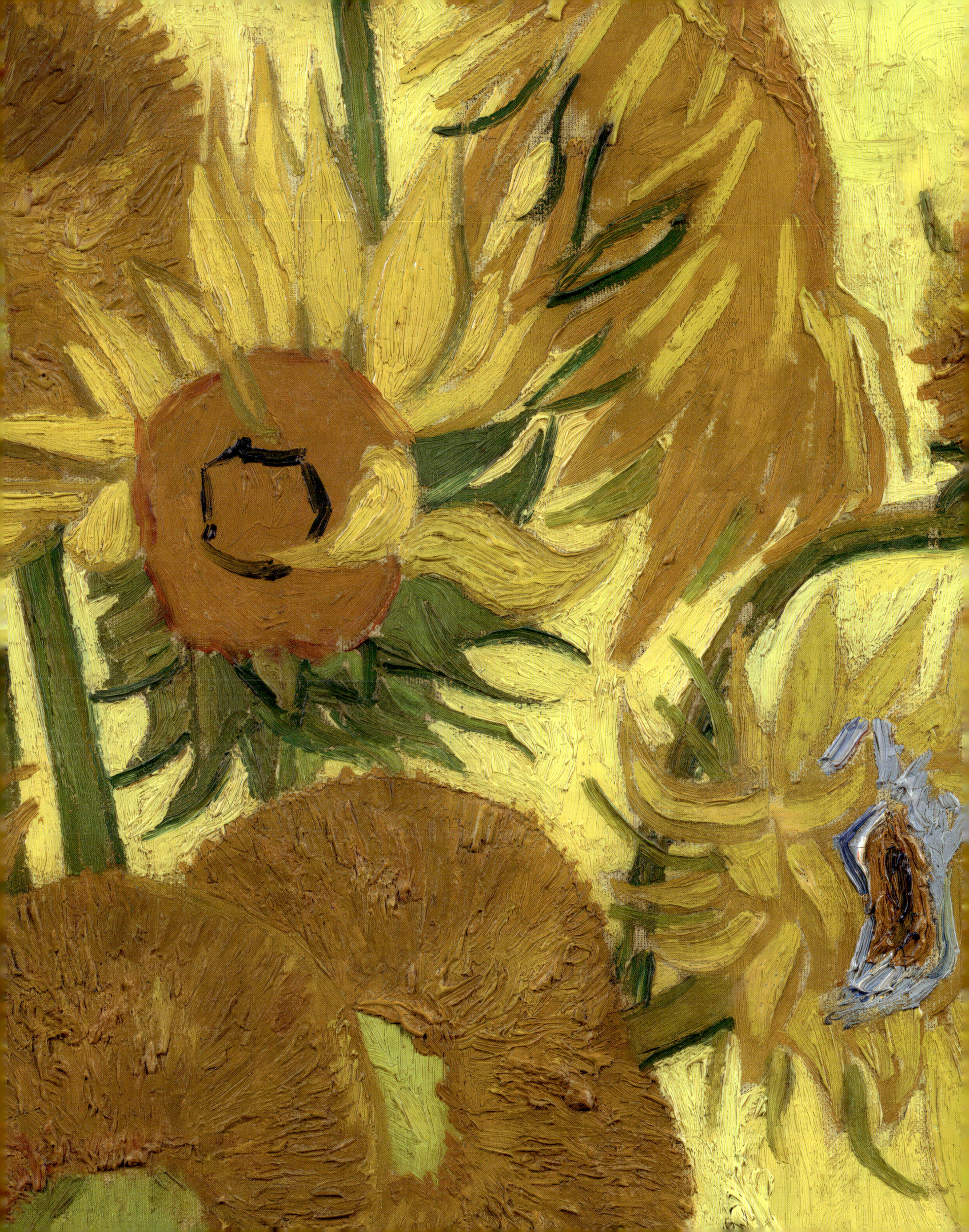

"To be sufficiently heated up to melt those golds and those flower tones, not just anybody can do that, it takes an individual's whole and entire energy and attention."

—Vincent van Gogh to Theo van Gogh
January 22, 1889

Painting in Blue and Yellow

—*Jennifer A. Thompson*

In a single week in August 1888, Vincent van Gogh painted four sunflower pictures, vertical canvases dominated by yellow and orange bouquets silhouetted against resplendent green, royal blue, turquoise, or yellow backgrounds (see *figs. 2, 31*; see also pp. 10–11, 14–15). Seven letters written that week offer insight into his motivation and glimpses of his creative process.[1] Today the ubiquity of these sunflower paintings makes them feel inevitable and obscures their initial role as exercises in color and brushwork intended to decorate the modest building in the Provençal city of Arles that housed Van Gogh's studio. Encouraged by Paul Gauguin's reaction to the canvases and intent on new decorative schemes, Van Gogh returned to sunflowers five months later, embarking on a winter painting campaign infused with memory and shaped by conversations with Gauguin (see Shields's essay in this volume). In the months that followed, he repeatedly revisited the canvases, imagining how they might be framed and presented, and positioning them at the center of his artistic practice.

In the Studio

Writing to fellow artist Émile Bernard from Arles on or about Tuesday, August 21, 1888, Van Gogh reported, "I'm thinking of decorating my studio with half a dozen paintings of *Sunflowers*."[2] The previous year while living in Paris, the thirty-five-year-old artist had used still-life painting to experiment with color.[3] Among the eighty-odd still lifes he produced in the Montmartre apartment he shared with his younger brother Theo were four horizontal paintings of dried sunflower heads lying on a table (*fig. 1*). The complementary colors and lively patterns of stippling, dots, dashes, and hatched lines on these canvases reveal an artist grappling with the innovative approaches of the Impressionists and Neo-Impressionists. These efforts to modernize and find a style of his own were installed in the summer of 1887 at the Café du Tambourin, a local restaurant. That fall, two of them were praised by Gauguin, who selected them as part of an exchange of artwork.[4]

Despite the abundant flora present in and around Arles, where Van Gogh moved in February 1888, he did not explore

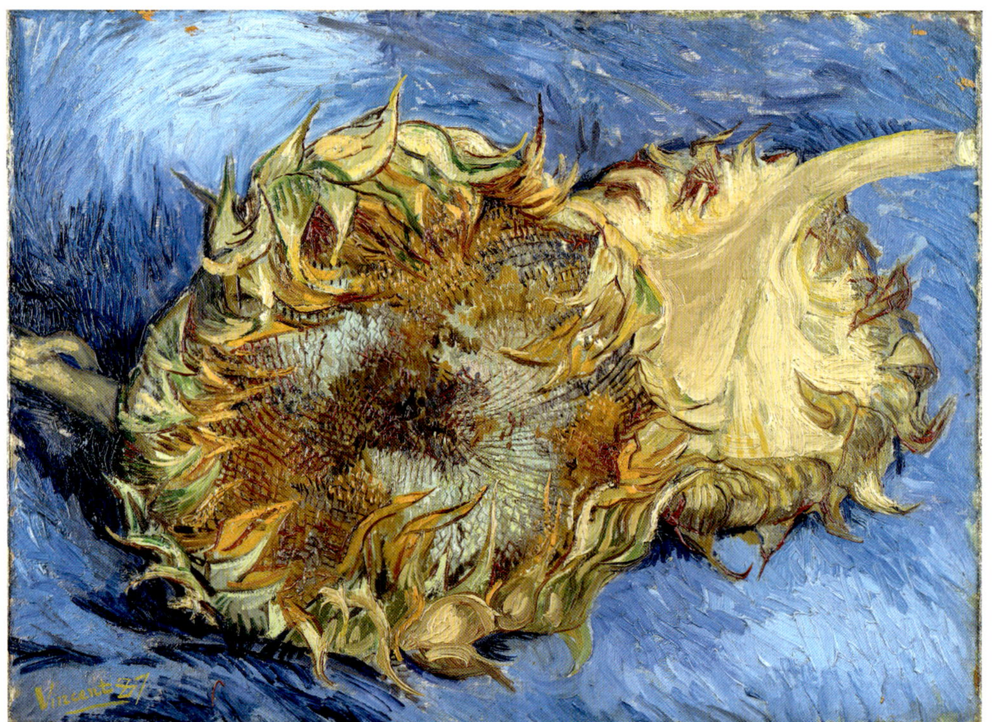

Fig. 1
Vincent van Gogh (Dutch, 1853–1890)
Sunflowers
Paris, August–September 1887
Oil on canvas
17 × 24 in. (43.2 × 61 cm)
The Metropolitan Museum of Art, New York: Rogers Fund, 1949, 49.41

floral subjects that spring or early summer. In August he lamented this oversight in a letter to Theo: "I'm annoyed with myself for not painting flowers here."[5] A few weeks later, when a model was unavailable and relentless summer mistrals made painting outdoors difficult, he turned his attention to the local vegetation then in full array.

The resumption of flower painting after nearly a year's hiatus involved two pictures of a colorful majolica jug filled with oleanders (*figs. 3, 4*).[6] In one, a sprawling top-heavy arrangement casts a lilac shadow over a table and two books below, a suggestive domestic tableau like several Van Gogh had made in Arles in the spring (see *figs. 28, 29*). The other adopts an uneasy downward view onto the vase. A crisp line delineates the light-colored table surface from a mid-tone blue wall, suggesting that Van Gogh was no longer seeking to represent a realistic setting but to evoke the nature of a flower associated with the Mediterranean region and with amorous feelings. Indeed, he wrote to Theo around this time that "instead of trying to render exactly what I have before my eyes, I use colour more arbitrarily in order to express myself forcefully."[7] The flat picture planes, intense color combinations, increasing monumentality, and portrait-like quality of the oleanders parallel what he would soon do with sunflowers.

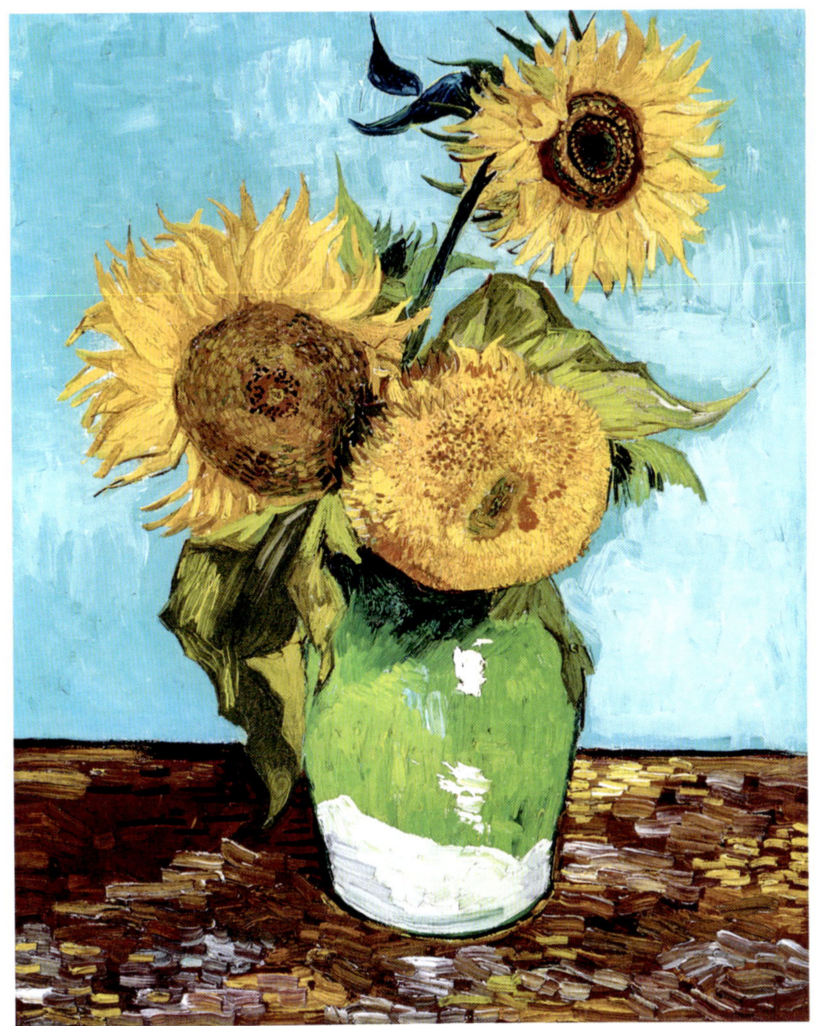

Fig. 2
Vincent van Gogh
Sunflowers
Arles, August 1888
Oil on canvas
28¾ × 22¹³⁄₁₆ in. (73 × 58 cm)
Private collection

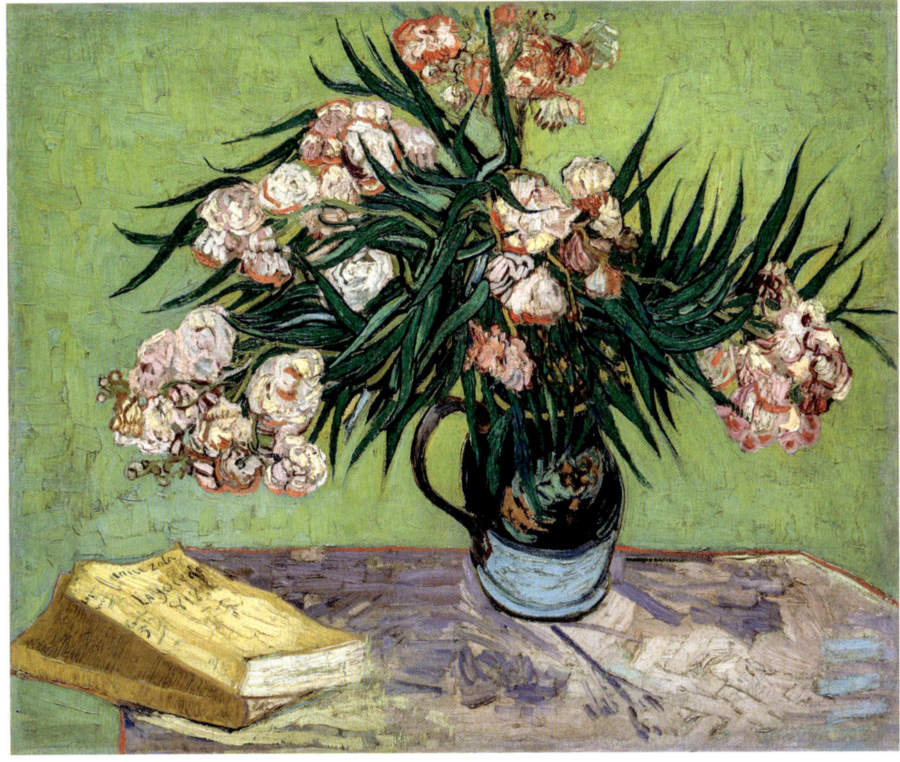

Fig. 3
Vincent van Gogh
Oleanders
Arles, August 1888
Oil on canvas
23¾ × 29 in. (60.3 × 73.7 cm)
The Metropolitan Museum of Art, New York: Gift of Mr. and Mrs. John L. Loeb, 1962, 62.24

By August 22, Van Gogh reported to Theo that he was working on three canvases of sunflowers every day starting at sunrise "because the flowers wilt quickly and it's a matter of doing the whole thing in one go."[8] It is difficult to track individual sunflowers across the paintings, and he must have procured fresh ones as the week advanced. As the bouquet expanded, from three to fifteen blooms, so too did the size of his pictures. His initial efforts were on modest no. 20 (73 × 60 cm) and no. 25 (81 × 65 cm) canvases, common sizes for landscape paintings and studies.[9] His move to no. 30 canvases (92 × 73 cm)—which he might have stretched with portraits in mind—signals his confidence and growing ambitions for the sunflower paintings. At odds with the increasing scale of his bouquets is the rustic half-glazed earthenware pot in which they are presented. Martin Bailey has observed that the flowers would have been too tall and too heavy to stand in such a vessel—a type commonly used in Provence for storing food—and that Van Gogh's pictures fictively imagine them in these humble containers.[10]

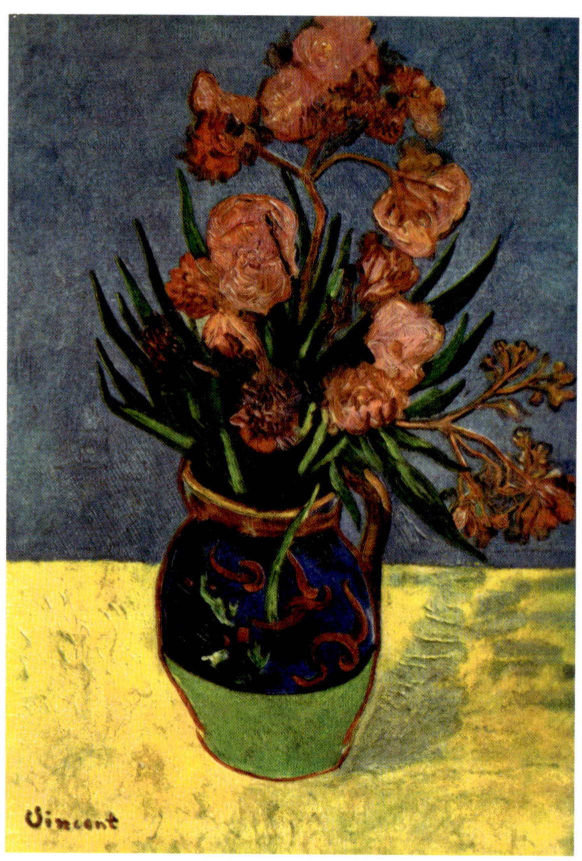

Fig. 4
Vincent van Gogh
Oleanders
Arles, August 1888
Oil on canvas
22¹⁄₁₆ × 14³⁄₁₆ in. (56 × 36 cm)
Location unknown

Unlike the uniform sunflowers in Claude Monet's 1881 bouquet (see *fig. 16*), Van Gogh's blooms are at different life stages, ranging from diminutive buds and flowers brimming with fluffy petals to blossoms laden with seeds and shedding leaves.[11] Their individual and varied features suggest they came from a flower garden rather than a cultivated patch where plants would come into bloom at the same moment. In fact, Van Gogh, using pencil, reed pen, and brush, drew a dense panoply of sunflowers in the garden of a bathhouse in early August 1888 (*fig. 5*). Located not far from his studio, the garden might have supplied the flowers and an approach for the paintings. Van Gogh's pen picks out the sunflowers, some with dark round eyes and radial petals, others with dotted or seeded centers, anticipating what he would do in paint two weeks later.[12]

In his return to the sunflower, Van Gogh had two artists firmly in mind: Édouard Manet and Adolphe Monticelli. Twice that week he asked Theo to recall a painting they had seen together two years earlier, in 1886, in the auction rooms of the Hôtel Drouot in Paris: "Do you remember . . . we saw a quite extraordinary Manet, some large pink peonies and their green leaves on a light background?"[13]

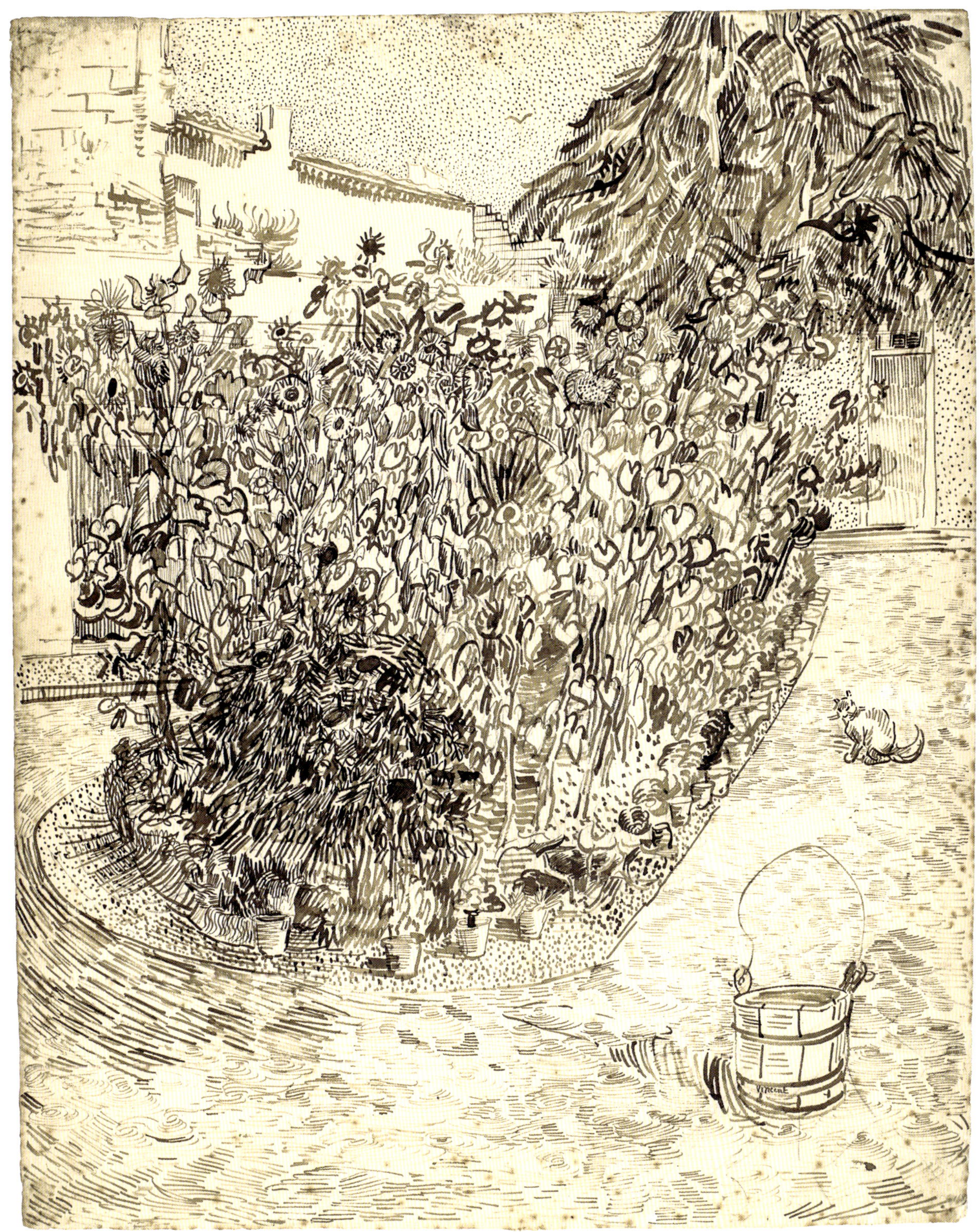

Fig. 5
Vincent van Gogh
Garden of a Bathhouse
Arles, August 1888
Pencil, reed pen, and brush and ink on paper
23⅞ × 19⅜ in. (60.7 × 49.2 cm)
Van Gogh Museum, Amsterdam
(Vincent van Gogh Foundation)

Painted on a size 30 canvas, Manet's peonies and their greenery are luminous and velvety (*fig. 6*). Praising the picture's harmony and the way the French artist captured the essence of the flower, Van Gogh called attention twice to the composition's radiant buff-colored ground. By the time he mentioned Manet's painting to Theo, he had embarked on a large-scale sunflower canvas with a yellow ground (see pp. 10–11), reprising a color arrangement he first attempted in Paris (see *fig. 27*).

Concurrently, Van Gogh admired the brilliant colors and textures of Monticelli's still lifes. Urging his sister Willemien, who was then visiting Theo in Paris, to study a Monticelli still life owned by her two brothers (*fig. 7*), he praised the "painter who did the south all in yellow, all in orange, all in sulphur" before describing the sunflower painting on his easel and boasting, "I expect one day to exhibit that one in Marseille."[14]

Van Gogh's interest in and admiration for Monticelli underpinned much of his time in Arles, fifty-six miles northwest of the older artist's native city of Marseille. In Paris the Van Gogh brothers and the Scottish art dealer Alexander Reid developed a conviction that the paintings of the recently deceased Monticelli were underappreciated and began to buy them as investments. Theo acquired six Monticellis; sold others on behalf of his employer, the gallery Boussod, Valadon & Cie; and helped to publish an album of lithographs and texts on Monticelli.[15] In a sign of support for this joint enterprise, one of Van Gogh's first stops upon arriving in Arles was to visit an antique shop to inquire about buying Monticelli works in the area.[16]

Monticelli's struggles with poverty, alcohol, and mental health issues no doubt reverberated with Van Gogh. Recognizing Monticelli's understanding of color and vigorous application of paint as signs of considerable energy, concentration, and effort, Van Gogh objected to the opinion that the Marseillais artist was a slovenly drunkard and felt he had been unfairly maligned. Describing himself as a son or brother of Monticelli, Van Gogh acquired a second-hand black velvet jacket and straw hat like those Monticelli wore and wrote that he would wear them when he and Gauguin visited Marseille.[17] That excursion never happened, but the promise of it and the prospect of carrying on

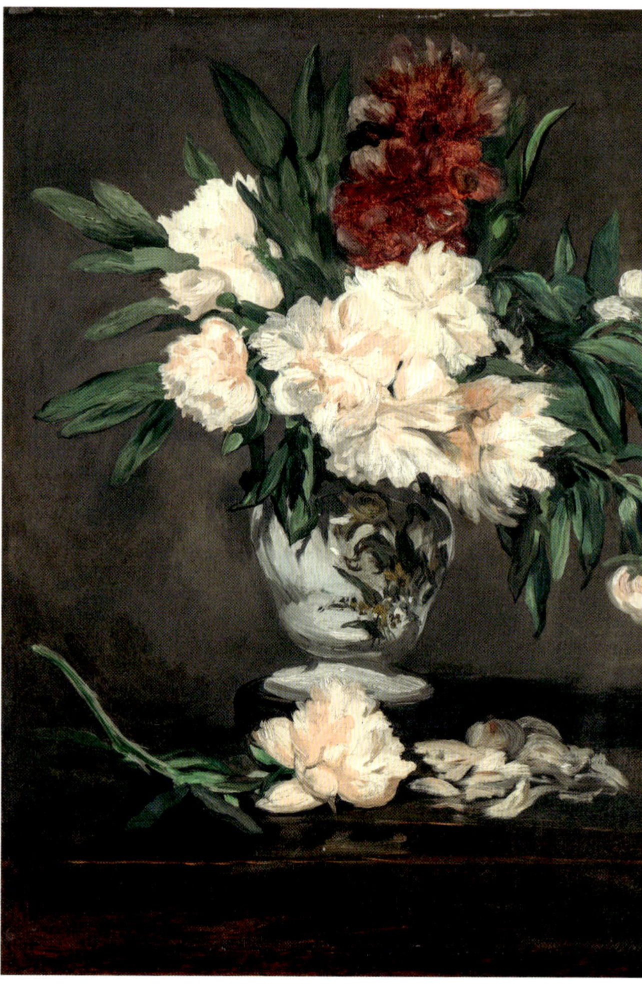

Fig. 6
Édouard Manet (French, 1832–1883)
Vase of Peonies on a Pedestal
1864
Oil on canvas
36¾ × 27⁹⁄₁₆ in. (93.3 × 70 cm)
Musée d'Orsay, Paris: Donation Étienne Moreau-Nélaton, 1906, RF 1669

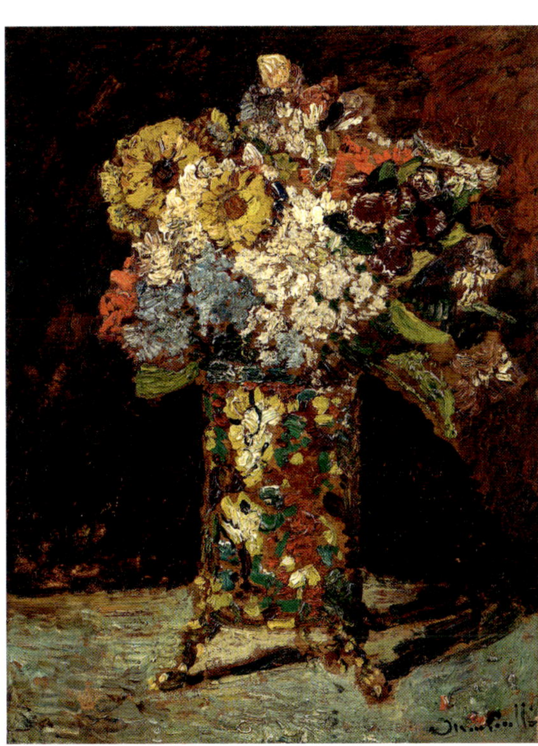

Fig. 7
Adolphe Monticelli (French, 1824–1886)
Vase of Flowers
c. 1875
Oil on panel
20¹⁄₁₆ × 15³⁄₈ in. (51 × 39 cm)
Van Gogh Museum, Amsterdam
(Vincent van Gogh Foundation)

Monticelli's color work and impastoed surfaces guided his work on the *Sunflowers*.

Van Gogh was fond of describing Monticelli's encrusted paint surfaces as "barbotine," comparing them to a pottery-decorating technique in which a mixture of clay and water known as slip is used to create textured patterns.[18] In Van Gogh's *Sunflowers*, the thickly painted flowers stand out in relief next to more thinly applied stems and backgrounds. That he was intentionally building up the flowers with pigment is suggested in a midweek letter concerned with the consistency of his paints. He pressed Theo to ask if Tasset & L'Hôte, a preferred Paris art supply shop, would consider making paint from coarsely ground pigments using a limited amount of oil. He imagined that this mixture would result in fresher colors, rougher textures, and possibly financial savings.[19]

Van Gogh's first accounts of the *Sunflowers* focus on color: "Harsh or broken yellows will burst against various BLUE backgrounds, from the palest Veronese to royal blue."[20] At least four yellows were used on the canvases alongside a variety of blues to create what he described as "a symphony in blue and yellow."[21] Equating color with music, vibration, and feeling was a common trope in the late nineteenth century and would have felt especially applicable to flower painting, in which there is no narrative, only color and form. As Van Gogh explained to his sister, "One can speak poetry just by arranging colours well, just as one can say comforting things in music."[22] Van Gogh's color experiments may have begun with twisting together strands of brightly dyed wool. Bernard first noticed wool balls in the artist's Paris studio, and their survival today attests to the foundational role of color in Van Gogh's practice (*fig. 8*).[23] Equally, the artist's habit of making closely related still lifes, albeit with radically different palettes, helps to explain the multiple pictures of shoes, books, crabs, apples, and quinces in his oeuvre, works in which color dramatically alters the mood.

Decorating with Sunflowers

Pleased with the four canvases drying in his studio, Van Gogh began to imagine them not in his workspace but decorating a spare room upstairs. After a string of excuses and delays, Gauguin had finally committed to a timeline for leaving the Breton town of Pont-Aven and joining Van Gogh in Arles. Inspired by his colleague's imminent arrival and conscious of his earlier appreciation for sunflowers, Van Gogh moved the larger sunflower canvases upstairs and planned to install them alongside four size 30 landscapes, a daunting array for a room measuring roughly nine by eleven feet and containing two windows and an aslant wall.[24]

From the start, the *Sunflowers* were integral to the artist's efforts to decorate the rental property.[25] In fact, he began the August week obsessing over finances and complaining of boarding-house life. His letters to Theo pitch the idea of making the rental property habitable and include a plea for 300 francs to purchase beds, linens, and chairs. Drawing on an inheritance, Theo sent the requested funds in early September, and the building on the place Lamartine began its transformation into the Yellow House, a home and studio invested with Van Gogh's dreams of an artists' community in the South.[26]

Although Van Gogh painted three views of his own bedroom (see *fig. 33*), no representation of the adjacent guest room survives to indicate the atmosphere he hoped to create there. In early September he described the room to Theo: "You'll see these big paintings of . . . sunflowers stuffed into this tiny little boudoir with a pretty bed and everything else elegant. It won't be commonplace."[27] Unlike his Impressionist peers, for whom decoration was often site-specific and planned in advance, Van Gogh approached the decoration of the Yellow House as a modular exercise capable of variation and achieving impact through its totality. Art historian Roland Dorn has proposed that Van Gogh imagined as many as thirty-five pictures—depicting sunflowers, portraits, landscapes, garden views, and a nearby café—decorating the Yellow House.[28] Nearly all were places and people associated with Arles, intensely local canvases whose proximity inside the modest structure would, the artist imagined, enhance their color contrasts and dialogue

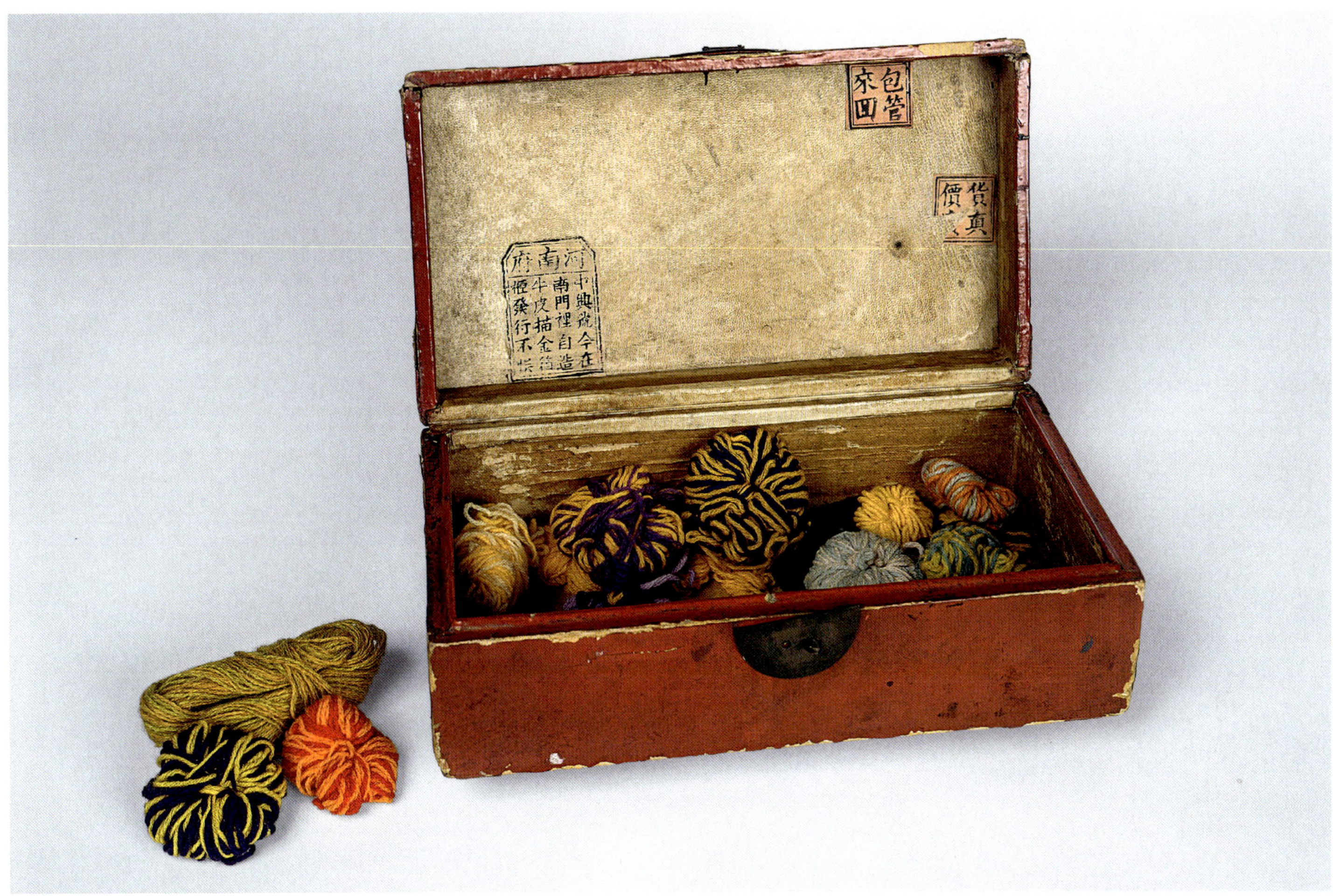

Fig. 8
Vincent van Gogh's red lacquered box containing sixteen small balls of wool
Box: 4 5/16 × 11 13/16 × 6 5/16 in. (11 × 30 × 16 cm)
Van Gogh Museum, Amsterdam
(Vincent van Gogh Foundation)

with one another. By painting predominantly on size 30 canvases, a scale better suited to a gallery or a wealthy patron's home, Van Gogh embraced the juxtaposition of large paintings in small rooms as a model of contrasts—big and small, sweet and savory—that he uniquely associated with Japan (see Contractor's essay in this volume, pp. 88–89).[29]

Given the dominant, almost confrontational presence of the sunflower paintings in the guest bedroom, it is striking that neither Gauguin nor Theo immediately responded to them. Almost a week after Gauguin's arrival in Arles in October 1888, Van Gogh reported to his brother that he had yet to learn what his friend thought of the decoration, and when Theo came in December, his own silence necessitated the needling prompt from his brother: "When you visited I think you must have noticed in Gauguin's room the two no. 30 canvases of the sunflowers."[30] In time, Gauguin would admit that he liked Van Gogh's sunflower paintings better than Monet's, and Theo in turn began entertaining his brother's plans to debut the canvases in Paris in early 1889.[31]

“Two of Them, Exactly the Same”

In January 1889, Gauguin unabashedly wrote to claim one of Van Gogh’s canvases: “Your sunflowers on a yellow background . . . I regard as a perfect page of an essential ‘Vincent’ style.”[32] Three weeks earlier, he had departed Arles in a rush, leaving his friend hospitalized for a mutilated earlobe and in the midst of a mental health crisis. Irritated and unwilling to give up any of his *Sunflowers*, Van Gogh vowed to make two more “exactly the same.”[33] Seven days later he confirmed as much in a letter to Theo: “I’ve just put the finishing touches to the absolutely equivalent and identical repetitions” (see pp. 22–23, 26–27).[34]

With no sunflowers to be had in the middle of the winter, Van Gogh used the August paintings as a guide and relied on memory and imagination, the very subjects of the “electric” debate between Van Gogh and Gauguin in the fall (see Shields’s essay in this volume). Along with the new pair, he produced another picture, likely made in December, of the yellow-on-yellow sunflowers painted on a coarse canvas of the type favored by Gauguin (see pp. 18–19).[35] The December and January canvases are close in scale, palette, and composition to the August versions, but none of the works is identical to another.[36] Amplifying color contrasts, abstracting forms, and making each bloom ever more itself, Van Gogh created recognizable yet distinct variants. A prominent way in which the repetitions diverge from their August progenitors is apparent in the exaggerated red and blue centers of flowers near the middle right of the January paintings.

In the August pale-blue-ground picture, the corresponding flower’s center is burgundy with a dark nucleus inside an incomplete circle (see pp. 14–17). It harmonizes with the rest of the painting and is accompanied by an angular leaf that extends almost to the canvas edge. In the painting’s January variant, the flower’s interior is worked with geranium lake and orange pigments blended wet-on-wet in sweeping arcs (opposite; see also pp. 22–23). A glob of brown paint is ringed by a spattering of impastoed gold dots that represent seeds. These features make this bloom into a stylized flower whose vibrant color, even though dulled by time, draws the eye.[37] Its accompanying leaf is a thinly painted arabesque.

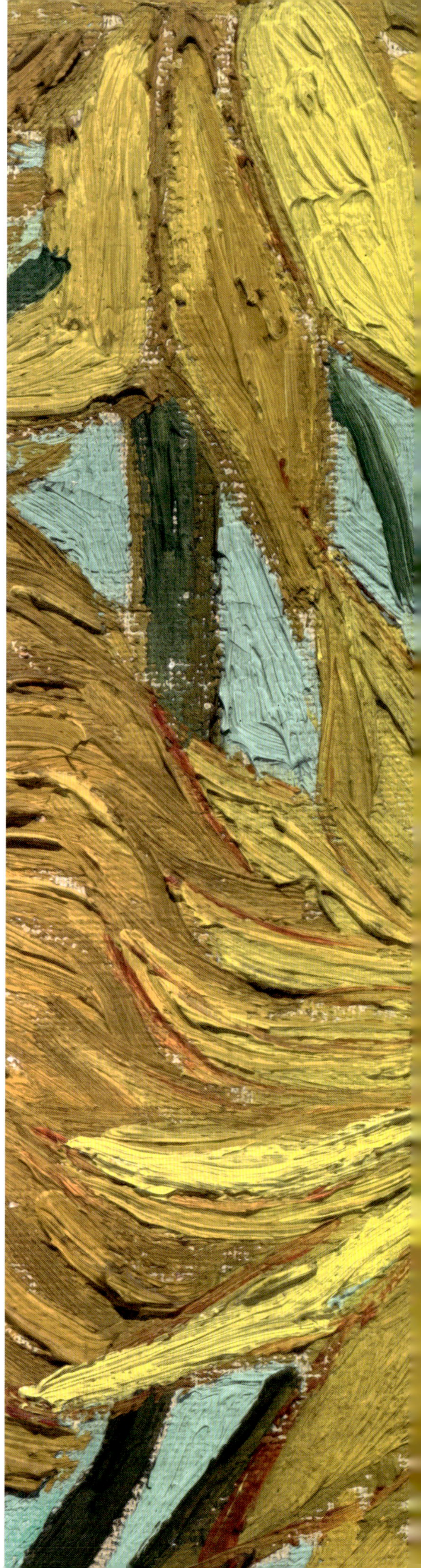

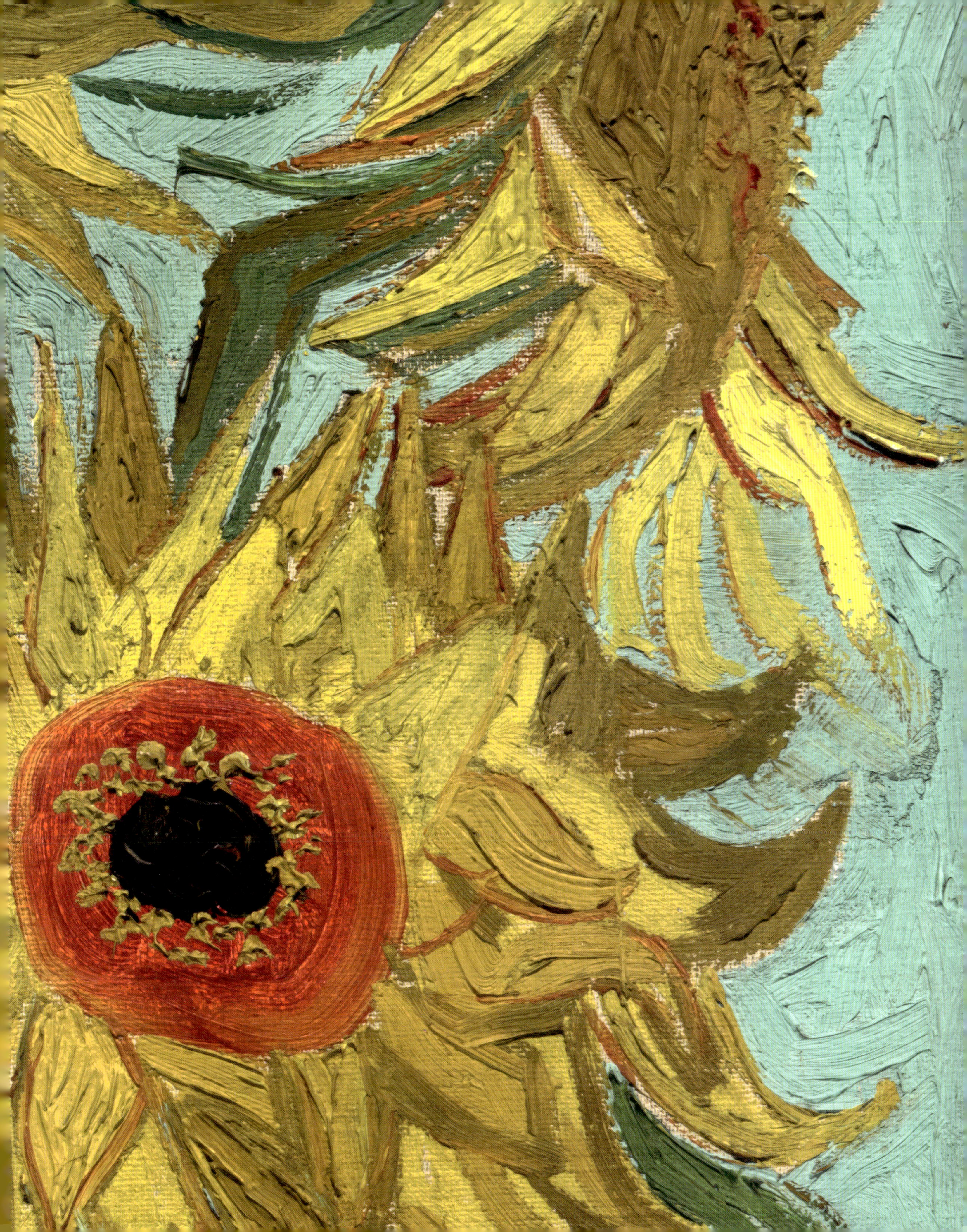

Similarly, the yellow-background *Sunflowers* has a new addition in the melting blue eye (or is it a gaping mouth?) of the corresponding flower at center right (see pp. 26–29). Such unrealistic poetic flourishes make for vivacious pictures and help to position them as pairs.

Recent investigation of the Philadelphia painting has identified what appear to be charcoal lines around one of the uppermost sunflower heads, suggesting that Van Gogh drew a few key elements before laying in the main forms with thin paint.[38] He left areas untouched or in reserve around each blossom save for the dangling flower on the right, which was painted over a thin turquoise-blue layer. Flower stems and petals were worked next in bright yellows and greens, followed by the thickly painted flower heads—each composed of its own system of dots, dabs, radial lines, and comma-shaped strokes—that stand out from the canvas like a sculpted relief. At a later stage Van Gogh returned to the blue-green background, layering vertical and horizontal brushstrokes in a woven pattern. The upper part of the vase is a highly constructed arrangement that suggests light falling on the round shoulder of the vessel, at odds with the lilac lower half worked with wet, smeary strokes filling in the space between the orange contour lines. The deep red "Vincent" (Van Gogh knew his last name was hard for many to pronounce) borrows the highlight color of the unusually textured lobed sunflower at center left.[39]

With the repetitions and a growing realization that he would have to leave the Yellow House, Van Gogh began to consider other arrangements and venues for the *Sunflowers*. In late January 1889, he assembled two triptychs in his studio and showed them to his friend the postman Joseph Roulin. Pairs of sunflower pictures that Van Gogh described as "yellow shutters" or "candelabra" flanked portraits of Roulin's wife in the guise of *la berceuse* (the cradle rocker) (see *fig. 36*). The postman's reaction to these ensembles, which Van Gogh imagined consoling fishermen at sea, is unknown, and the exercise, sketched in a May letter to Theo (see *fig. 37*), was not repeated (see Contractor's essay in this volume, pp. 90–94).[40]

In early May 1889, when Van Gogh's mental health necessitated his entry into an asylum fifteen miles away,

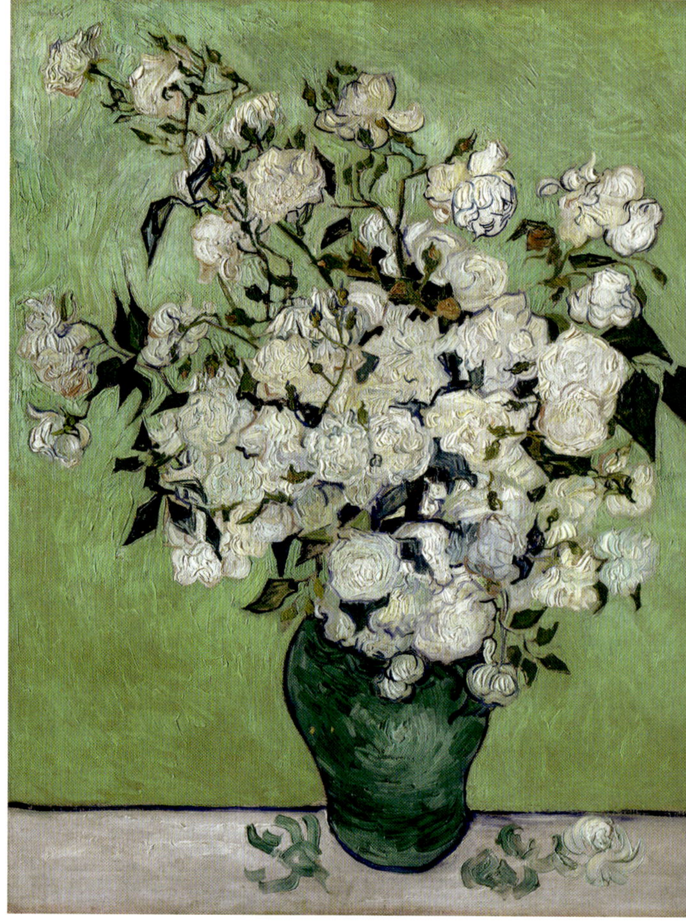

Fig. 9
Vincent van Gogh
Roses
Saint-Rémy-de-Provence, May 1890
Oil on canvas
36⅝ × 29⅛ in. (93 × 74 cm)
The Metropolitan Museum of Art, New York: The Walter H. and Leonore Annenberg Collection, Gift of Walter H. and Leonore Annenberg, 1993, Bequest of Walter H. Annenberg, 2002, 1993.400.5

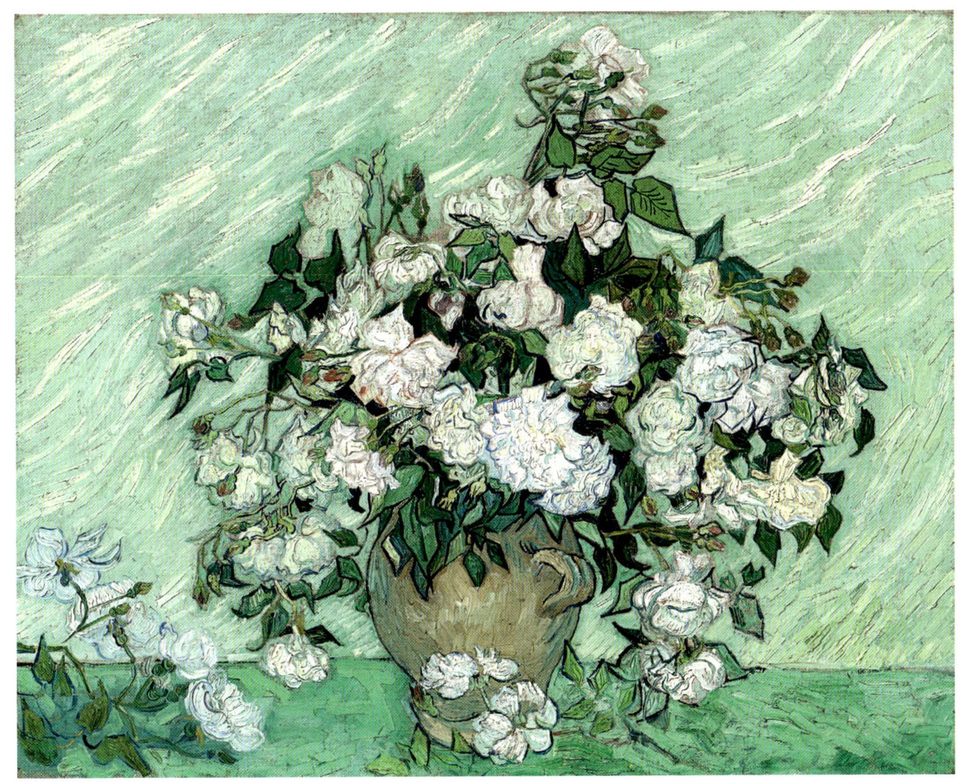

Fig. 10
Vincent van Gogh
Roses
Saint-Rémy-de-Provence, May 1890
Oil on canvas
$27\frac{15}{16} \times 35\frac{7}{16}$ in. (71 × 90 cm)
National Gallery of Art, Washington, DC: Gift of Pamela Harriman in memory of W. Averell Harriman, 1991.67.1

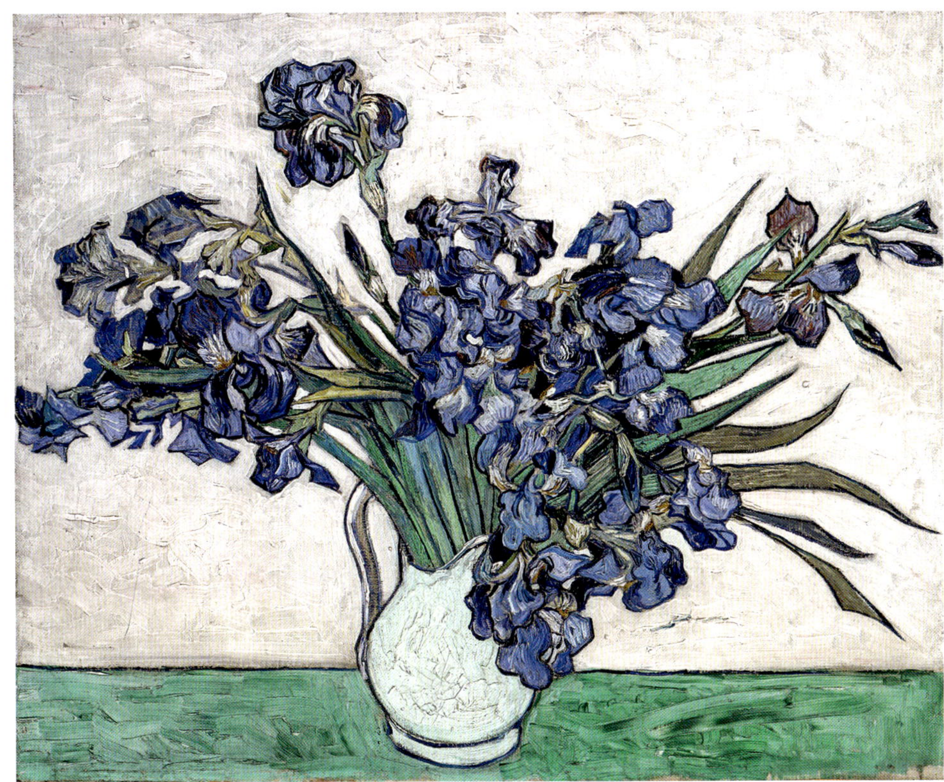

Fig. 11
Vincent van Gogh
Irises
Saint-Rémy-de-Provence, May 1890
Oil on canvas
$29 \times 36\frac{1}{4}$ in. (73.7 × 92.1 cm)
The Metropolitan Museum of Art, New York: Gift of Adele R. Levy, 1958, 58.187

in Saint-Rémy-de-Provence, he sent the *Sunflowers* to Theo, having earlier authorized him to show two at his Paris gallery from time to time.[41] Instead, Theo kept them tucked away, unsure what his bourgeois clients, much less his employer, would think of such melted surfaces. One hung above the mantel in his apartment, where it was seen by close friends and had, as Theo described, "the effect of a piece of fabric embroidered with satin and gold, it's magnificent."[42] Theo lent two to Julien Tanguy, the Paris color merchant who supplied Van Gogh and other avant-garde artists with materials and occasionally showed their work in his shop. "The Sunflowers were on show at Tanguy's this week and made a very good effect," Theo reported in December. "Your paintings cheer up Tanguy's shop, and *père* Tanguy likes them a lot."[43] There, artists and critics got a look at the *Sunflowers*, and soon afterward the first critical review of Van Gogh's work appeared in a Parisian publication.

In the article, the French poet and art critic Albert Aurier characterized Van Gogh as a dreamer whose "strange, intense, feverish works" were filled with notions of and a search for truth and simplicity. Aurier singled out "the sumptuous sunflower, which [Van Gogh] repeats tirelessly, like a monomaniac, how can one explain it if one refuses to admit his persistent preoccupation with some vague and glorious heliomythic allegory?"[44] Calling the artist a Symbolist, Aurier was convinced that ideas lie behind the tangible forms in his paintings, a reading Van Gogh resisted, insisting to Aurier that the sunflowers convey "gratitude."[45] Despite a long tradition of sunflowers being associated with light, love, and Christ due to the flower's habit of turning toward the sun, he shied away from such symbolism.[46]

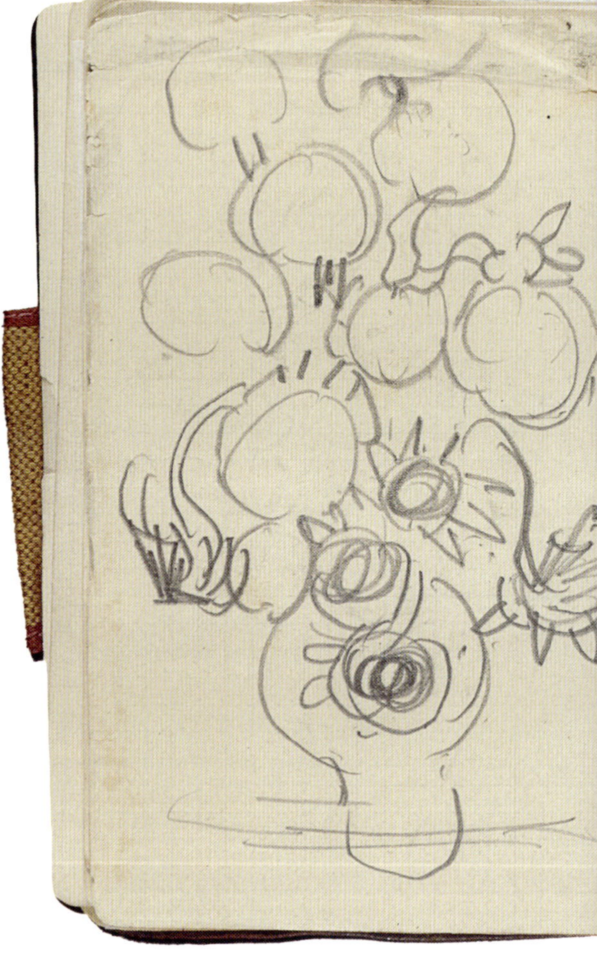

Aurier's article provided advance publicity for the debut of Van Gogh's work with Les Vingt, a group of young artists who exhibited annually in Brussels. Offered a four-meter-long wall for the display of his paintings in January 1890, Van Gogh proposed to show two sunflower pictures and four landscapes.[47] Dorn has observed that the orange- and yellow-colored sunflowers would have been complemented by Provençal scenes painted predominantly in blue, violet, red, and green, thereby creating a color wheel.[48] Even in the more progressive environment of Les Vingt, a fuss was made over the *Sunflowers* when Belgian artist Henry de Groux refused to participate in the exhibition, writing to art critic Octave Maus that he was "not wishing . . . to find myself in the same room as the laughable vase of sunflowers by Mr Vincent, or by any other *agent provocateur*."[49] Van Gogh's friends came to his defense, and he sold *The Red Vineyards at Arles* (1888; Pushkin State Museum of Fine Arts, Moscow), one of the few sales made in his lifetime.[50]

In May 1890, as he was preparing to move north to Auvers-sur-Oise, Van Gogh returned with a "frenzy" to flowers painted on size 30 canvases.[51] The process of packing his possessions, the arrival of a fresh shipment of canvas and paints, and his imminent departure from the lush terrain of the South resulted in a focused week of work. This time he painted irises and roses in fat-bellied pots and pitchers (*figs. 9–11, 13*). In these unruly compositions in which blooms spill out, bouquets dwarf their vessels, greens compete with pulsing pinks, and punchy purples with yellows, Van Gogh seemed determined to restage one of his Provençal successes.[52] Undertaken in an ecstatic burst that nearly delayed his planned departure, the canvases demonstrate the artist's reengagement with flower painting as a vehicle for bold color combinations (sadly, his determined use of geranium lake pigments has left the once-vibrant pink colors in these paintings susceptible to fading). Not conceived as pendant pairs, instead they might have been configured as horizontal and vertical sets of flowers. The potential commercial appeal of such works was not lost on Van Gogh, as Nienke Bakker has suggested, since the artist wished to compensate his brother for the moving expenses incurred that month.[53] Though the pictures would not be sold in his lifetime, the art market might have been on his mind a few weeks later in Auvers when he drew sunflowers on facing pages of a sketchbook (*fig. 12*). Intending to use the printing press owned by Dr. Paul Gachet, his physician and friend, to create a series of etchings of Provençal subjects, he might have imagined the bouquets bundled into a commercial offering not unlike the album made for Monticelli.[54]

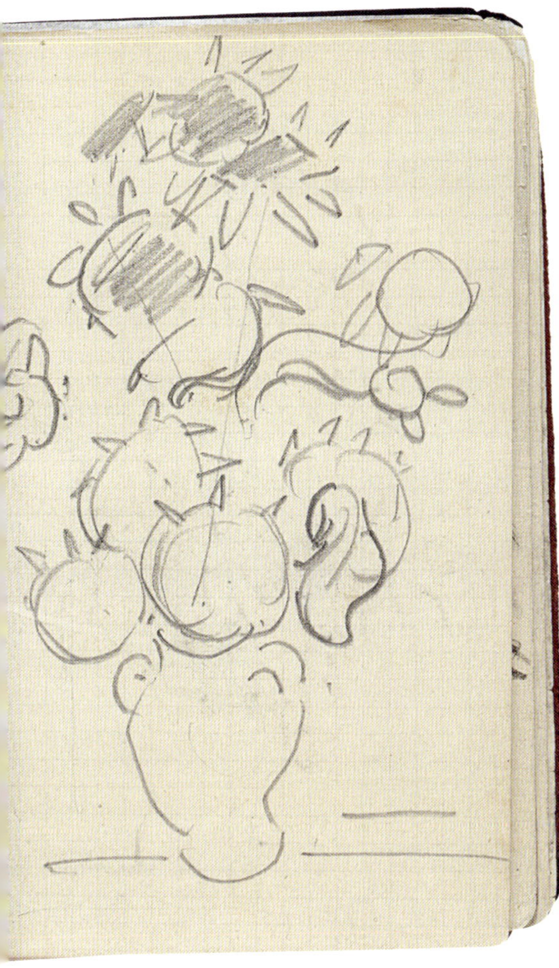

Fig. 12
Vincent van Gogh
Sunflowers (left and right)
From a Paris and Auvers-sur-Oise sketchbook, May–July 1890
Graphite on paper
Each page: 5¼ × 3⅜ in. (13.4 × 8.5 cm)
Van Gogh Museum, Amsterdam
(Vincent van Gogh Foundation)

Van Gogh's two-year sojourn in the South of France helped to develop his distinctive language of color and

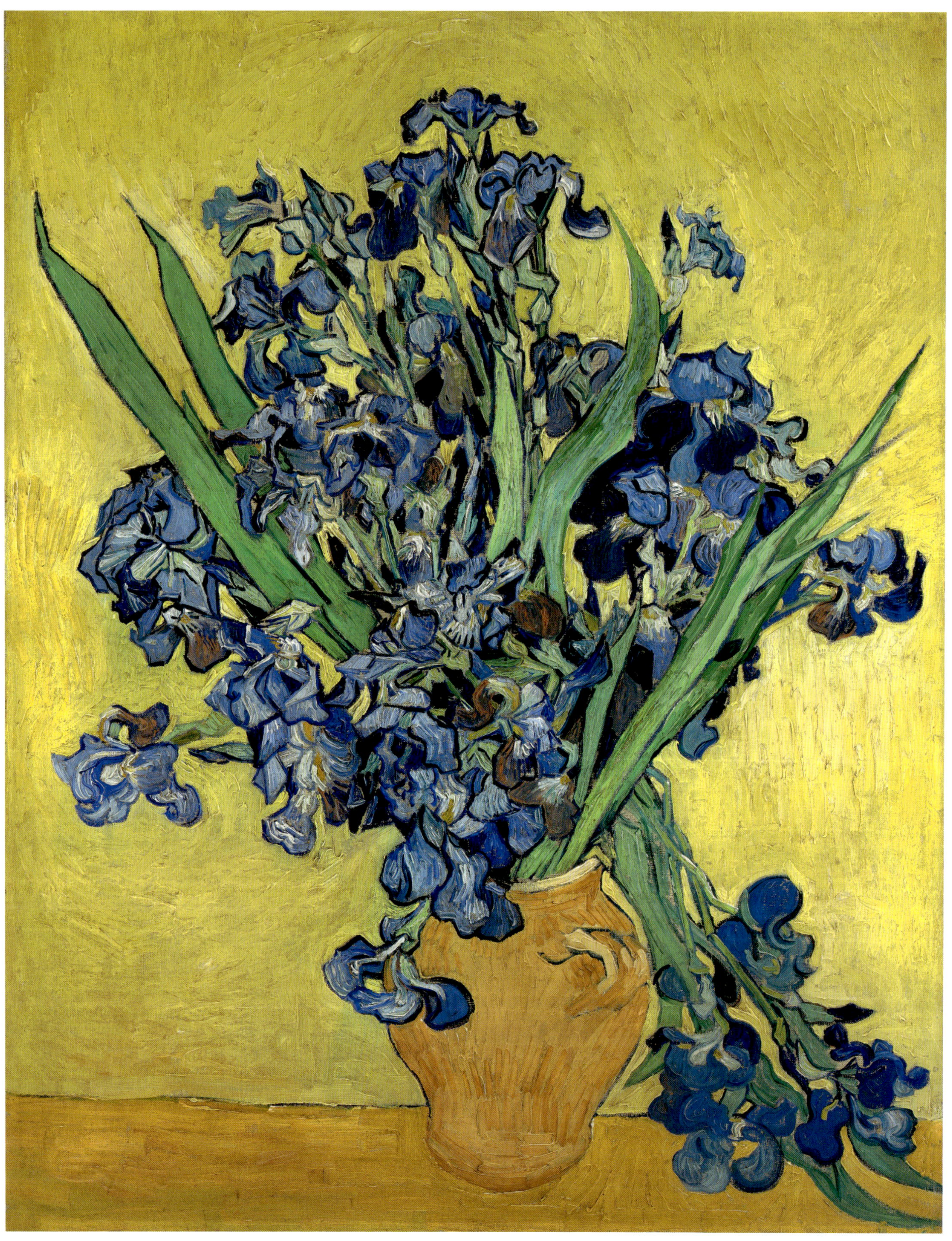

brushwork, and he learned there "to paint in such a way that if it comes to it, everyone who has eyes could understand it."[55] The passion and creativity he invested in painting sunflowers and imagining the encounters others would have with the canvases after they left his studio have positioned them uniquely in his oeuvre. Created during a week in which he ate well, painted with the gusto of a Marseillais eating bouillabaisse, and began to conceive of his studio as a home and artistic community, the *Sunflowers* have come to be seen as a turning point in the artist's search for a style. Van Gogh's vision and touch are inescapable on their surfaces. The success of the *Sunflowers* in conveying the essence of sunshine, of life and gratitude, and of Van Gogh himself was universally recognized by his friends and family. On July 30, 1890, when Theo, Émile Bernard, Julien Tanguy, Dr. Gachet, and others gathered at Van Gogh's funeral in Auvers, the artist's coffin was reverently adorned with yellow flowers, including "the sunflowers he loved so much."[56]

Fig. 13
Vincent van Gogh
Irises
Saint-Rémy-de-Provence, May 1890
Oil on canvas
36½ × 29$\frac{1}{16}$ in. (92.7 × 73.9 cm)
Van Gogh Museum, Amsterdam
(Vincent van Gogh Foundation)

For their expertise and generous assistance, I am grateful to Barbara Buckley, Tara Contractor, Kate Duffy, Colin Fanning, Christopher Ferguson, Katie Hanson, Cornelia Homburg, Teresa Lignelli, Aleksandra Popowich, Christopher Riopelle, Caroline Shields, Anya Shutova, Mark Tucker, Jeffrey Werner, and Jason Wierzbicki.

1. Vincent van Gogh to Theo van Gogh, Arles, August 19 or 20, 1888, letter 664; Vincent van Gogh to Émile Bernard, Arles, on or about August 21, 1888, letter 665; Vincent van Gogh to Theo van Gogh, Arles, August 21 or 22, 1888, letter 666; Vincent van Gogh to Willemien van Gogh, Arles, August 21 or 22, 1888, letter 667; Vincent van Gogh to Theo van Gogh, Arles, August 23 or 24, 1888, letter 668; Vincent van Gogh to Theo van Gogh, Arles, August 26, 1888, letter 669; and Vincent van Gogh to Willemien van Gogh, Arles, on or about August 26, 1888, letter 670. All correspondence to or from Van Gogh cited herein is from *Vincent van Gogh: The Letters*, ed. Leo Jansen, Hans Luijten, and Nienke Bakker (Van Gogh Museum & Huygens ING, 2009), online version December 2024, https://vangoghletters.org/. This essay's opening quotation is from Vincent van Gogh to Theo van Gogh, Arles, January 22, 1889, letter 741.
2. Van Gogh to Bernard, Arles, on or about August 21, 1888, letter 665.
3. On his still-life practice, see Laura Coyle, "The Still-Life Paintings of Vincent van Gogh and Their Context" (PhD diss., Princeton University, 2007).
4. On the Café du Tambourin display, see Vincent van Gogh to Theo van Gogh, Paris, between about July 17 and 19, 1887, letter 571, esp. nn2–3. For the exchange of artworks between Van Gogh and Gauguin, see Douglas W. Druick and Peter Kort Zegers, *Van Gogh and Gauguin: The Studio of the South*, exh. cat. (Art Institute of Chicago, 2001), 82.
5. Vincent van Gogh to Theo van Gogh, Arles, August 8, 1888, letter 657.
6. The oleander still lifes have been variously dated to August and September 1888. Around August 13 of that year, Van Gogh wrote to Theo that he hoped "to do a study of oleanders in the next few days"; Vincent van Gogh to Theo van Gogh, Arles, on or about August 13, 1888, letter 660.
7. Vincent van Gogh to Theo van Gogh, Arles, August 18, 1888, letter 663.
8. Vincent van Gogh to Theo van Gogh, Arles, August 21 or 22, 1888, letter 666.
9. Van Gogh stretched his own canvases, cutting pieces from a ten-meter roll of commercially prepared linen and attaching them to standard-size stretcher frames; see Ella Hendriks, "Sunflowers Up Close," in Nienke Bakker and Ella Hendriks, *Van Gogh and the Sunflowers: A Masterpiece Examined*, exh. cat. (Van Gogh Museum, 2019), 57–59. See also Jansen, Luijten, and Bakker, *Vincent van Gogh: The Letters*, letter 666, n2.
10. Martin Bailey, *The Sunflowers Are Mine: The Story of Van Gogh's Masterpiece* (Frances Lincoln, 2013), 10, 17–18. For the Impressionists' preference for humble earthenware pots, see Audrey Gay-Mazuel, "Ceramic Containers in French Nineteenth-Century Flower Painting," in *Working Among Flowers: Floral Still-Life Painting in Nineteenth-Century France*, ed. Heather MacDonald and Mitchell Merling, exh. cat. (Dallas Museum of Art, 2014), 50.
11. Monet's *Bouquet of Sunflowers* (1881; see *fig. 16*) was exhibited in New York in 1886 at the American Art Galleries from April 10 to 25, and then at the National Academy of Design from May 25 to June 30. They were sold that year to Colorado businessman Alden Wyman Kingman. Unfamiliar to Van Gogh, they were known to Gauguin; see Vincent van Gogh to Theo van Gogh, Arles, on or about November 19, 1888, letter 721 ("Gauguin was telling me the other day—that he'd seen a painting by Claude Monet of sunflowers in a large Japanese vase, very fine").
12. Van Gogh explained to Theo that if the drawing looked "too stiff," it was because it contained "information for painting"; Vincent van Gogh to Theo van Gogh, Arles, August 8, 1888, letter 657. For the likely location of the bathhouse, see Marije Vellekoop and Roelie Zwikker, *Arles, Saint-Rémy & Auvers-sur-Oise, 1888–1890*, vol. 4, *Vincent van Gogh Drawings*, ed. Sjraar van Heugten, Marije Vellekoop, and Roelie Zwikker (Van Gogh Museum, 2007), 153–57.
13. Vincent van Gogh to Theo van Gogh, Arles, August 23 or 24, 1888, letter 668; see also Vincent van Gogh to Theo van Gogh, Arles, August 26, 1888, letter 669.
14. Vincent van Gogh to Willemien van Gogh, Arles, on or about August 26, 1888, letter 670.
15. Aaron Sheon, "Theo van Gogh, Publisher: The Monticelli Album," *Van Gogh Museum Journal*, 2000, pp. 58–59, accessed August 20, 2025, https://www.dbnl.org/tekst/_van012200001_01/_van012200001_01_0007.php.
16. For this and other connections between Van Gogh and Monticelli, see Martin Bailey, "Van Gogh et Marseille: L'impossible voyage," in *Van Gogh–Monticelli*, exh. cat., Centre de le Vielle Charité, Marseille (Réunion des Musées Nationaux, 2008), 129–35.
17. Vincent van Gogh to Willemien van Gogh, Arles, on or about August 26, 1888, letter 670.
18. Vincent van Gogh to Theo van Gogh, Arles, August 18, 1888, letter 663; and Vincent van Gogh to Willemien van Gogh, Arles, on or about August 26, 1888, letter 670.
19. Vincent van Gogh to Theo van Gogh, Arles, August 23 or 24, 1888, letter 668.
20. Van Gogh to Bernard, Arles, on or about August 21, 1888, letter 665 (emphasis in original).
21. Vincent van Gogh to Theo van Gogh, Arles, August 21 or 22, 1888, letter 666. For the colors used in the sunflower paintings, see Hendriks, "Sunflowers Up Close," 63.

22. Vincent van Gogh to Willemien van Gogh, on or about November 12, 1888, letter 720. For more on this topic, see Natascha Veldhorst, *Van Gogh and Music: A Symphony in Blue and Yellow*, trans. Diane Webb (Yale University Press, 2018).
23. Laura Coyle, "Strands Interlacing: Colour Theory, Education and Play in the Work of Vincent van Gogh," *Van Gogh Museum Journal*, 1996, p. 119, accessed August 20, 2025, https://www.dbnl.org/tekst/_van012199601_01/_van012199601_01_0010.php.
24. For a blueprint of the house, see Roland Dorn, *Décoration: Vincent van Goghs Werkreihe für das Gelbe Haus in Arles* (Georg Olms Verlag, 1990), pls. XVIII and XIX.
25. For discussion and different perspectives on Van Gogh and decoration, see Dorn, *Décoration*; Cindy Kang, "Van Gogh's *Décoration*: Sources of Inspiration," and Marnin Young, "'Unity Is Strength': Van Gogh and the Exhibitions of the Avant-Garde," both in *Van Gogh: Poets & Lovers*, ed. Cornelia Homburg and Christopher Riopelle, exh. cat. (National Gallery Global, 2024), 133–42 and 119–28, respectively; and David J. Getsy, "Exalting the Unremarkable: Van Gogh's Poet's Garden and Gauguin's Bedroom," in *Van Gogh's Bedrooms*, ed. Gloria Groom, exh. cat. (Art Institute of Chicago, 2016), 37–49.
26. Van Gogh's monthly allowance from his brother averaged 250 francs. For Van Gogh's financial plans, see Vincent van Gogh to Theo van Gogh, Arles, August 19 or 20, 1888, letter 664; Arles, September 8, 1888, letter 676; and Arles, September 9, 1888, letter 677.
27. Vincent van Gogh to Theo van Gogh, Arles, September 9, 1888, letter 677.
28. Dorn, *Décoration*, 334–475.
29. Vincent van Gogh to Willemien van Gogh, Arles, September 9 and about September 14, 1888, letter 678.
30. Vincent van Gogh to Theo van Gogh, Arles, on or about October 29, 1888, letter 715; and Arles, January 28, 1889, letter 743.
31. See Vincent van Gogh to Theo van Gogh, Arles, on or about November 19, 1888, letter 721; and Arles, January 22, 1889, letter 741; and Theo van Gogh to Vincent van Gogh, Paris, May 21, 1889, letter 774.
32. Gauguin to Van Gogh, Paris, between January 8 and 16, 1889, letter 734.
33. Vincent van Gogh to Paul Gauguin, Arles, January 21, 1889, letter 739.
34. Vincent van Gogh to Theo van Gogh, Arles, January 28, 1889, letter 743.
35. For a compelling analysis of the ways the painting relates to the other yellow versions, see Nienke Bakker and Christopher Riopelle, "The *Sunflowers* in Perspective," in *Van Gogh's Sunflowers Illuminated: Art Meets Science*, ed. Ella Hendriks and Marije Vellekoop (Amsterdam University Press, 2019), 31. On the painting's dating, see Shields's essay in this volume, p. 63.
36. Van Gogh's practice of making repetitions was the subject of a 2013 exhibition; for the exhibition catalogue, see Eliza E. Rathbone et al., eds., *Van Gogh Repetitions*, exh. cat., Phillips Collection, Washington, DC (Yale University Press, 2013), esp. Marcia Steele and Elizabeth Steele, "Methods for Making Repetitions," 170–77.
37. Van Gogh knew that geranium and red lake pigments would fade, and he applied the red-pink color generously hoping to compensate. For a discussion of these pigments and how they have altered in his paintings, see Inge Fielder et al., "Materials, Intention, and Evolution," in Groom, *Van Gogh's Bedrooms*, 86–91.
38. There are traces of charcoal in unpainted areas surrounding the round head, third from the left in the top row of flowers. Additional charcoal marks may be covered by paint. This feature is consistent with the Amsterdam version painted the same week; see Ashok Roy and Ella Hendriks, "Van Gogh's 'Sunflowers' in London and Amsterdam," *National Gallery Technical Bulletin* 37 (2016): 64. I am grateful to my colleagues Kate Duffy, Teresa Lignelli, Aleksandra Popowich, Mark Tucker, and Jason Wierzbicki for these and other observations.
39. For Van Gogh's decision to sign his works "Vincent," see Vincent van Gogh to Theo van Gogh, Arles, on or about March 25, 1888, letter 589.
40. Van Gogh's rapidly evolving ideas and enthusiasm for the *Sunflowers* play out over several letters to Gauguin and Theo between January and May 1889. In letters dating to late January, Van Gogh introduced the idea of the triptych being meant to console sailors (on this, see Contractor's essay in this volume, p. 92), referring to the sunflower pictures flanking portraits of Roulin's wife as "candelabra," and mentioned that he had shown the arrangement to Roulin. By May, Van Gogh referred to the *Sunflowers* as "yellow shutters," further embracing the idea of them as "wings" of an altarpiece. See Van Gogh to Gauguin, Arles, January 21, 1889, letter 739; and Vincent van Gogh to Theo van Gogh, Arles, January 28, 1889, letter 743; Arles, January 30, 1889, letter 744; and Saint-Rémy-de-Provence, on or about May 23, 1889, letter 776.
41. Vincent van Gogh to Theo van Gogh, Arles, January 22, 1889, letter 741; and Arles, May 2, 1889, letter 767.
42. Theo van Gogh to Vincent van Gogh, Paris, July 16, 1889, letter 792.
43. Theo van Gogh to Vincent van Gogh, Paris, December 22, 1889, letter 830.
44. G.-Albert Aurier, "Les isolés: Vincent van Gogh," *Le Mercure de France*, January 1890, pp. 24–29, trans. and repr. in Ronald Pickvance, *Van Gogh in Saint-Rémy and Auvers*, exh. cat. (Metropolitan Museum of Art, 1986), 310–25 (quotation on p. 313).
45. Vincent van Gogh to Albert Aurier, Saint-Rémy-de-Provence, February 9 or 10, 1890, letter 853.
46. For a discussion of the various meanings assigned to sunflowers, see Druick and Zegers, *Van Gogh and Gauguin*, 75–77.
47. Vincent van Gogh to Octave Maus, Saint-Rémy-de-Provence, November 20, 1889, letter 821.
48. Roland Dorn, "Vincent van Gogh's Concept of 'Décoration,'" in *Vincent van Gogh International Symposium*, ed. Takashina Shūji, Ronarudo Pikkubansu, and Arikawa Haruo (Tokyo Shimbun, 1988), 383.
49. Henry de Groux to Octave Maus, [1890], quoted in Jansen, Luijten, and Bakker, *Vincent van Gogh: The Letters*, letter 713, n4.
50. Simon Kelly, "'A Big, Good Enterprise': Van Gogh and His Markets," in *Becoming Van Gogh*, ed. Timothy J. Standring and Louis van Tilborgh, exh. cat. (Denver Art Museum, 2012), 65–66.
51. "But in the last few days at St-Rémy I worked like a man in a frenzy, especially on bouquets of flowers"; Vincent van Gogh to Willemien van Gogh, Auvers-sur-Oise, June 5, 1890, letter 879.
52. A potential sequence for these paintings is suggested by Eliza E. Rathbone, "Van Gogh's Late Still-Life Paintings: From Still to Life," in *Van Gogh: Still Lifes*, ed. Ortrud Westheider and Michael Philipp, exh. cat., Museum Barberini, Potsdam (Prestel, 2019), 94–97.
53. Nienke Bakker, "Charmed by Flowers," in *Van Gogh in Auvers-sur-Oise: His Final Months*, ed. Nienke Bakker et al., exh. cat., Van Gogh Museum, Amsterdam (Thames & Hudson, 2023), 81.
54. Vincent van Gogh to Theo van Gogh, Auvers-sur-Oise, June 17, 1890, letter 889.
55. Vincent van Gogh to Theo van Gogh, Arles, August 21 or 22, 1888, letter 666.
56. Bregje Gerritse and Sara Tas, "The First Signs of Recognition," in Bakker et al., *Van Gogh in Auvers-sur-Oise*, 183.

"Gauguin, in spite of himself and in spite of me, has proved to me a little that it was time for me to vary things a bit—I'm beginning to compose from memory."

—Vincent van Gogh to Theo van Gogh
On or about November 19, 1888

Still Life in the Studio of the South: Van Gogh, Gauguin, and Painting from Memory

—*Caroline Shields*

From October 23 to December 23, 1888, Vincent Van Gogh and Paul Gauguin lived and worked together in the southern French city of Arles—a period that Van Gogh described as *"excessively electric."*[1] In August, two months prior to Gauguin's arrival in Arles, Van Gogh was at work on his sunflower canvases, which culminated in two remarkably ambitious paintings that are arguably the most iconic still lifes in Western art (see pp. 10–11, 14–15). Bookending his and Gauguin's time together, Van Gogh created a second pair of equally astounding sunflower paintings in January 1889 (see pp. 22–23, 26–27). This essay positions the genre of still life as the catalyst for the explosive creativity and competition between the two artists that unfolded over the course of the two months they lived together. Notably, they rarely engaged with the genre during this otherwise highly productive period; Van Gogh and Gauguin painted at least fifty-eight canvases between them, only four of which were still lifes. Despite this relative paucity, in their portraits of each other made during this time, each depicted the other painting a still life (see *figs. 19, 21*). The genre of still life in general, and Van Gogh's sunflower paintings in particular, lies at the center of the debate that galvanized the two artists' exchange of ideas on the theory of painting from memory.

The Summer of 1888

The summer months leading up to Gauguin's arrival in Arles were a generative period for both Van Gogh and Gauguin. Van Gogh was in the midst of setting up his home and studio in what he called his "little yellow house" in Arles. He hoped that the Yellow House would become the site for his long-envisioned Studio of the South, where artists would gather to live and work together, finding inspiration in one another and in the brilliant sunlight of southern France.[2] Gauguin was living in the artists' colony of Pont-Aven in Brittany, where he and the painter Émile Bernard worked closely together. All three artists exchanged letters with one another, and these writings capture their thoughts and ideas. Of particular interest to each of them were theories of abstraction and painting from memory, which they referred to interchangeably with descriptions such as painting “from the imagination,” “with eyes half-closed,” or “dreaming before [nature].” Van Gogh and Gauguin frequently wrote that they would paint, compose, or draw *de tête*, a French expression that translates into English as “from memory” but literally means “from the head.”[3] In this practice, artists may observe a model—meaning any physical example, be it a person, a landscape, or a still life—but would purposefully not look at the model when it came time to paint their canvas. By contrast, the practice of directly referencing a model while painting is variously known as painting from the model, from life, after nature, or from observation.

For Van Gogh and Gauguin, memory and imagination were inextricably linked and together gave birth to creativity. While the relationship may not seem intuitive, the concept is in fact ancient. In Greek mythology, Mnemosyne, the goddess of memory, was the mother of the nine Muses. The human capacity to imagine is rooted in memory, and memory is itself a creative faculty of the mind.[4] Van Gogh and Gauguin intuited and explored this dynamic, finding inspiration in artists, poets, and scientists of their time.

Gauguin believed deeply that the path to realizing the highest form of art was through the process of painting from memory, whereas Van Gogh strongly preferred to paint from a model, and he composed his sunflower paintings in that way. That August, despite their different approaches, Van Gogh and Gauguin each created outstanding canvases in the still-life genre, and they took tremendous pride in their respective works. Eagerly awaiting Gauguin’s arrival in Arles, Van Gogh hung the sunflower paintings in the guest bedroom. When Gauguin walked into that room, he would have seen in those canvases an achievement in tune with, and perhaps even surpassing, the theoretical and aesthetic experimentation that he, too, had been exploring that summer.

Gauguin: Dreaming Before Nature

Gauguin's commitment to painting from memory stems from his conviction that this process leads to abstraction and a greater ability to move the viewer emotionally. In an 1885 letter to artist Émile Schuffenecker, Gauguin advised, "Above all, do not sweat over a painting; a great sentiment can be rendered immediately. Dream on it and look for the simplest form in which you can express it."[5] He further believed that the process heightened an artist's creative agency, as it relied upon their memory or imagination, rather than merely copying a model. Three years later, again writing to Schuffenecker, Gauguin offered, "Some advice: do not copy too closely after nature. Art is an abstraction; derive this abstraction from nature while dreaming before it, and think more about creation than the result."[6] For Gauguin, dreaming before nature meant metaphorically closing one's eyes before the model in order to conjure images from memory or the imagination.

Gauguin's belief that memory and imagination give way to abstraction and heightened emotional impact derived from diverse sources. In period science, he would have found a resonance with the idea that painting from memory allows artists to attain a more abstract quality in their art. The renowned French psychologist Théodule Ribot explained that, in memory, an image becomes a "transitional form between representation and pure concept that we now term a generic image."[7] Ribot's ideas appeared in a digested form in the popular periodical *Revue des deux mondes*, which Gauguin and Van Gogh regularly read and discussed.[8] In an 1885 article, philosopher Alfred Fouillée explained that the mind combines successive images into "a general and typical idea," continuing, "This spontaneous generalization is accomplished mechanically by the fusion of images in the memory."[9]

The writings of poet and art critic Charles Baudelaire were an important foundation for Gauguin in 1885 and again in the summer of 1888, when Bernard likely brought Baudelaire's writings with him to Pont-Aven.[10] Recent research by cognitive scientists illuminates the relationship between Baudelaire's and Gauguin's theories of memory. The studies show that, as Ribot and Gauguin anticipated, visual memory creates and stores "prototypical" or abstract

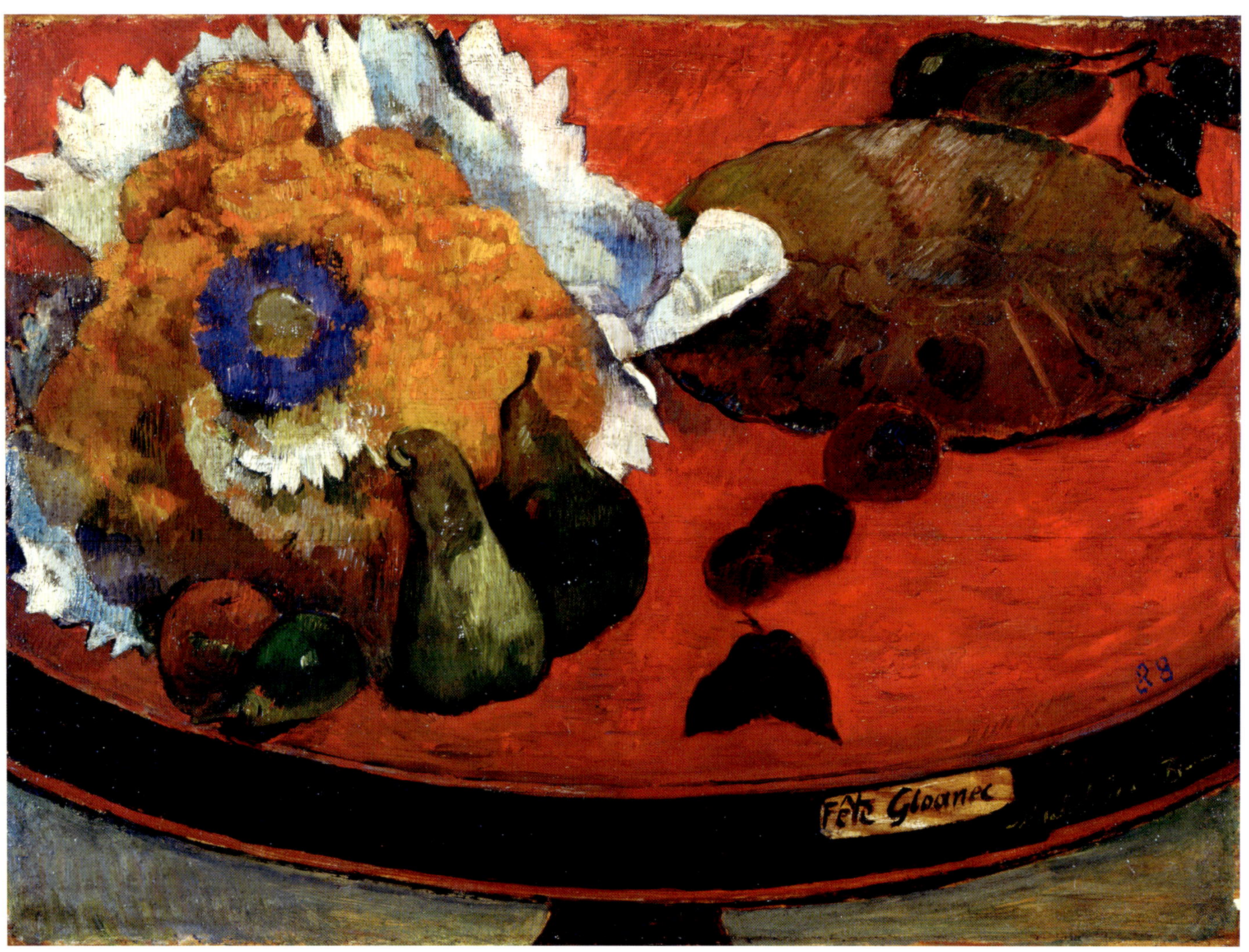

Fig. 14
Paul Gauguin (French, 1848–1903)
Still Life: Fête Gloanec
Pont-Aven, August 1888
Oil on panel
$19\frac{5}{16} \times 25\frac{11}{16}$ in. (49 × 65.3 cm)
Musée des Beaux-Arts d'Orléans, MO.64.1405

images, akin to Ribot's "generic" image. Further, the brain is more apt to recognize such an image, which it already has "on file," so to speak.[11] This science gives us a framework that helps to elucidate Baudelaire's assertion that "painting, which flows largely from the memory, appeals largely to the memory. The impact produced on the soul of the viewer is in direct relation to the means the artist uses."[12] That is, an artist who produces an image from memory eases the burden on the viewer's memory of recognizing that image. The passage appears in Baudelaire's chapter on the nineteenth-century French Romantic artist Eugène Delacroix, which Gauguin would have read with particular interest given his admiration for the artist's work and their shared focus on painting from memory. For Gauguin, this process was not just an aesthetic pursuit; rather profoundly, he understood its result, abstraction, as the most direct path to move and inspire his viewer through art.

Within days of his letter advising Schuffenecker to dream before nature, Gauguin painted *Still Life: Fête Gloanec* (1888; *fig. 14*), a picture that is widely recognized as a major step toward abstraction for the artist.[13] It is the first of several paintings in which Gauguin employed a single, bright background color that undermines any sense of three-dimensional space due to its lack of perspectival depth. The combination of different viewing angles from which he depicted the table, fruit, marigolds, and Breton tart heightens the spatial disorientation. Gauguin created *Still Life with Three Puppies* (1888; *fig. 15*) around the same time. The silhouetted forms, together with their strong outlines, are aesthetic properties that Gauguin associated with painting from memory.[14] As if to emphasize that this still life is imagined and not observed, the compositional space is entirely invented. The table, for example, appears to be viewed from above while the objects upon it are seen from the side. Similarly, while the puppies are immediately recognizable as puppies, they are in fact quite deformed. One senses that Gauguin was experimenting with the degree to which he could simplify and distort forms and still instantly evoke the essence of happy puppies lapping up milk. With both paintings, Gauguin insisted upon their inventiveness through distortions of space, form, and color, thereby claiming their creation as a product of his mind, and not a result of imitation.

Gauguin explored his theory of painting from memory explicitly through the genre of still life, a choice that simultaneously engaged with and defied the history of this genre. On the most practical level, still life is the easiest of all genres to paint from observation: A still-life model is affordable and disposable and stays still. It is quite remarkable to take the genre most easily painted from life yet insist instead upon painting the subject from memory. *Still Life with Three Puppies* calls attention to this apparent discrepancy between the potential ease of painting a still life from a model and Gauguin's refusal to do so.

Historically and through the nineteenth century, still life had been the quintessential genre for copying from nature and flaunting one's virtuosity in trompe l'oeil, meaning "to fool the eye."[15] This association dates back millennia, to a competition between two painters described in Pliny the Elder's *Natural History* (first century CE). After Zeuxis painted

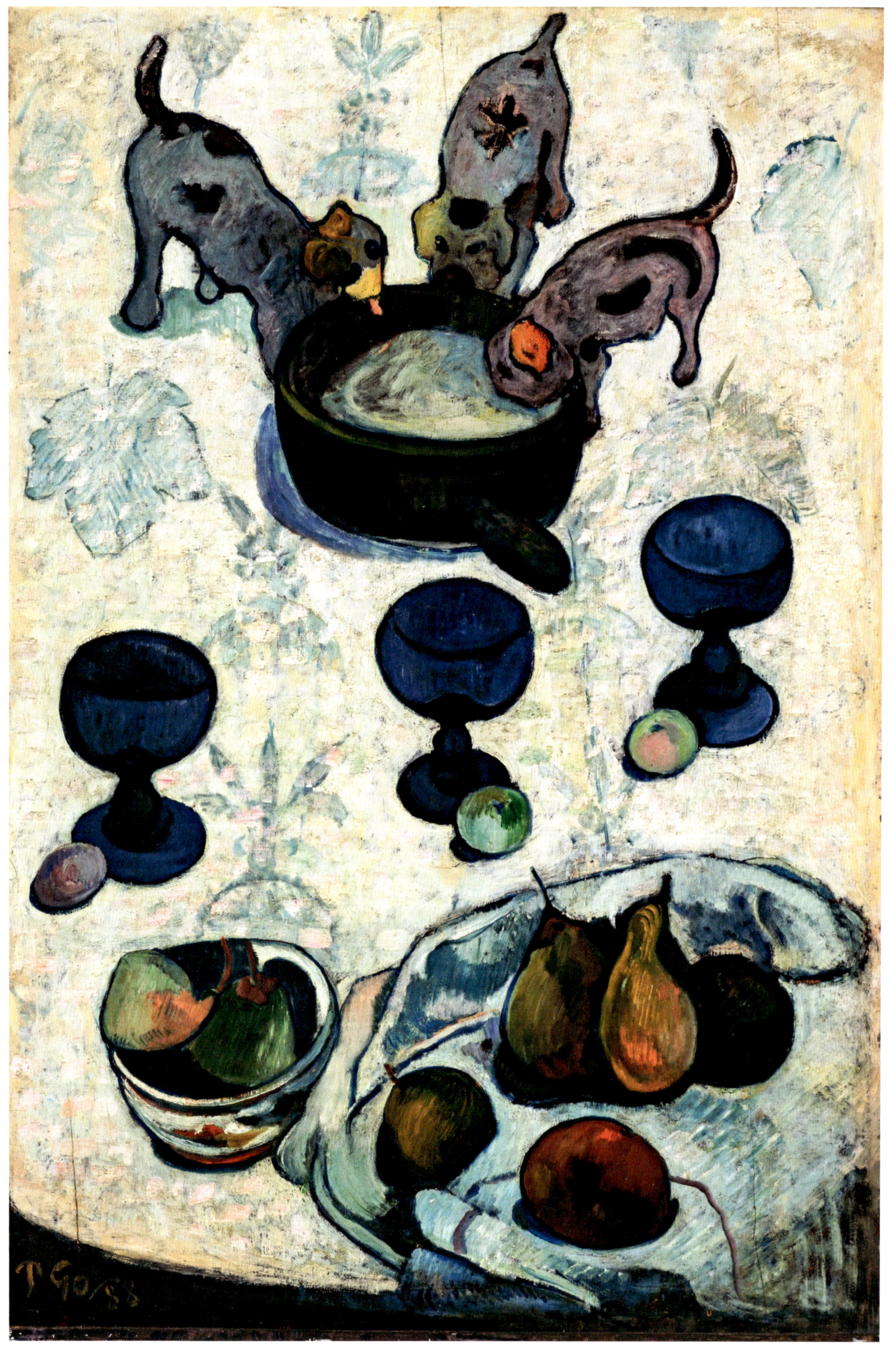
P Go/88

Fig. 15
Paul Gauguin
Still Life with Three Puppies
Pont-Aven, August 1888
Oil on panel
36⅛ × 24⅝ in. (92 × 63 cm)
The Museum of Modern Art, New York: Mrs. Simon Guggenheim Fund, 48.1952

grapes that proved so realistic they deceived birds, he asked Parrhasios, his competitor, to pull back the curtain on his own painting so that Zeuxis could see the picture behind it. The curtain, however, was itself the painting, and Zeuxis admitted that his opponent had accomplished the greater deception. Gauguin disdained such mindless mimesis of nature—and derided Zeuxis for it[16]—so when he painted the genre most famed and praised for such imitation, he undermined that quality by insisting upon working from memory instead.

Increasingly in the nineteenth century, counter to its association with copying, still life came to serve as an allegory of the creative process itself—an approach that aligned with Gauguin's aims. Gauguin thought deeply about the creative process and artistic freedom, and he expressed these views in his art and writing throughout his career.[17] The notion of achieving artistic liberty through still-life painting derives from the idea that artists have full creative control in crafting their pictures' models, from selecting the subject to arranging the components. In this sense, they compose each still life twice: once on the table, and again on the canvas.[18] Gauguin took this further by emphasizing the imaginary nature of his scenes through abstraction.

Van Gogh: Memory Versus Model

The concept of painting from memory was fraught for Van Gogh, as he felt strongly that he achieved his best work by painting from a model.[19] Van Gogh regularly struggled to find people to model for him, and when bad weather prevented him from painting landscapes outdoors, he felt he had few options to remain productive. During one stretch of rainy weather in September 1888, he wrote to his brother Theo, "If only I could draw figures from memory, I'd always have something to do."[20]

Despite his resistance in practice to painting from memory, Van Gogh grasped its theoretical implications and admired artists who followed the process. In April 1885, as he worked on *The Potato Eaters* (Van Gogh Museum, Amsterdam), he wrote to Theo:

> Still, it's coming along, and I think there'll be something very different in it from what you can

> ever have seen by me. At least that clearly.
> I mean the *life* especially. I'm painting this
> FROM MEMORY *on the painting itself.*
> But you know yourself how many times I've
> painted the heads!
> And furthermore I keep going and looking every evening, to redraw sections on the spot. But in the painting I let my own head, in the sense of *idea* or *imagination*, work, which isn't so much the case with *studies*, where no creative process *may* take place, but where one obtains *food* for one's imagination from reality so that it becomes right.

Remarkably, given that Van Gogh was still living in the Netherlands in 1885, he and Gauguin each arrived at this understanding of memory independently but from similar sources rooted in Delacroix's writings. Van Gogh continued in the same letter:

> It's the *second* time that I've derived a great deal from something Delacroix said.
> The first was his theory of colour, but I also read a conversation that he had with other painters about the making, that is the *creation*, of a painting.
> He asserted that one made the best paintings—from memory. *By heart!* he said.[21]

At this time Van Gogh was reading books by French art critic Charles Blanc, who, as Baudelaire did, derived his theories on painting from Delacroix's writings.[22]

The next time Van Gogh engaged meaningfully with the concept of painting from memory was in July 1888, when he expressed to Bernard:

> So, Rembrandt painted angels—he makes a portrait of himself as an old man, toothless, wrinkled, wearing a cotton cap—first, painting from life in a mirror—he dreams, dreams, and his brush begins his own portrait again, but from memory, and its expression becomes sadder and more saddening; he dreams, dreams on . . .
> I'm showing you a painter who dreams and who paints from the imagination.[23]

This language intermingling dreaming and memory echoes the letters Gauguin wrote to Schuffenecker in 1885 and 1888, quoted above. The ideas recurred for Van Gogh in different forms throughout the summer. In response to a now-lost letter from Van Gogh, Gauguin wrote to the Dutch artist:

> I've just read your interesting letter and I entirely agree with you on the slight importance that accuracy contributes to art.
>
> Art is an abstraction.[24]

Van Gogh conceived of the sunflower paintings amid this flurry of interest in memory, imagination, and abstraction during the summer of 1888. This marked a return to the sunflower, which he had explored a year before, between August and September 1887, in four canvases of cut flowers lying on a table (see *fig. 1*). Gauguin admired them and received two in exchange for one of his recent paintings.[25] Van Gogh was deeply hopeful that Gauguin would join him in Arles, which he believed would mark the start of his dream for the Yellow House to become an artists' haven. In filling the house with sunflower paintings,[26] he beckoned his friend to travel south. The weather that August had been unfavorable for a stretch of time, so a bouquet of freshly cut flowers indoors would have provided Van Gogh with a suitable model to work from.[27] Yet even with modest beginnings, Van Gogh conceived of these canvases as experiments in color and form from the outset (see *fig. 2*). As he enlarged his canvases and increased the number of sunflowers in them, the compositions became more and more impossible. Like Gauguin's *Still Life: Fête Gloanec* and *Still Life with Three Puppies* (both painted the same month as Van Gogh's August *Sunflowers*, though neither artist saw the other's work), these still lifes defy both reason and gravity, moving into the realm of imagination (see *fig. 31*). The sunflowers of the London and Munich canvases tower over their vases, which could not possibly have contained them (see pp. 10–11, 14–15).

With each successive sunflower canvas, Van Gogh further simplified his forms, culminating in the London painting. There the sunflowers appear in profile and silhouetted against the background with greater frequency, with strong contour

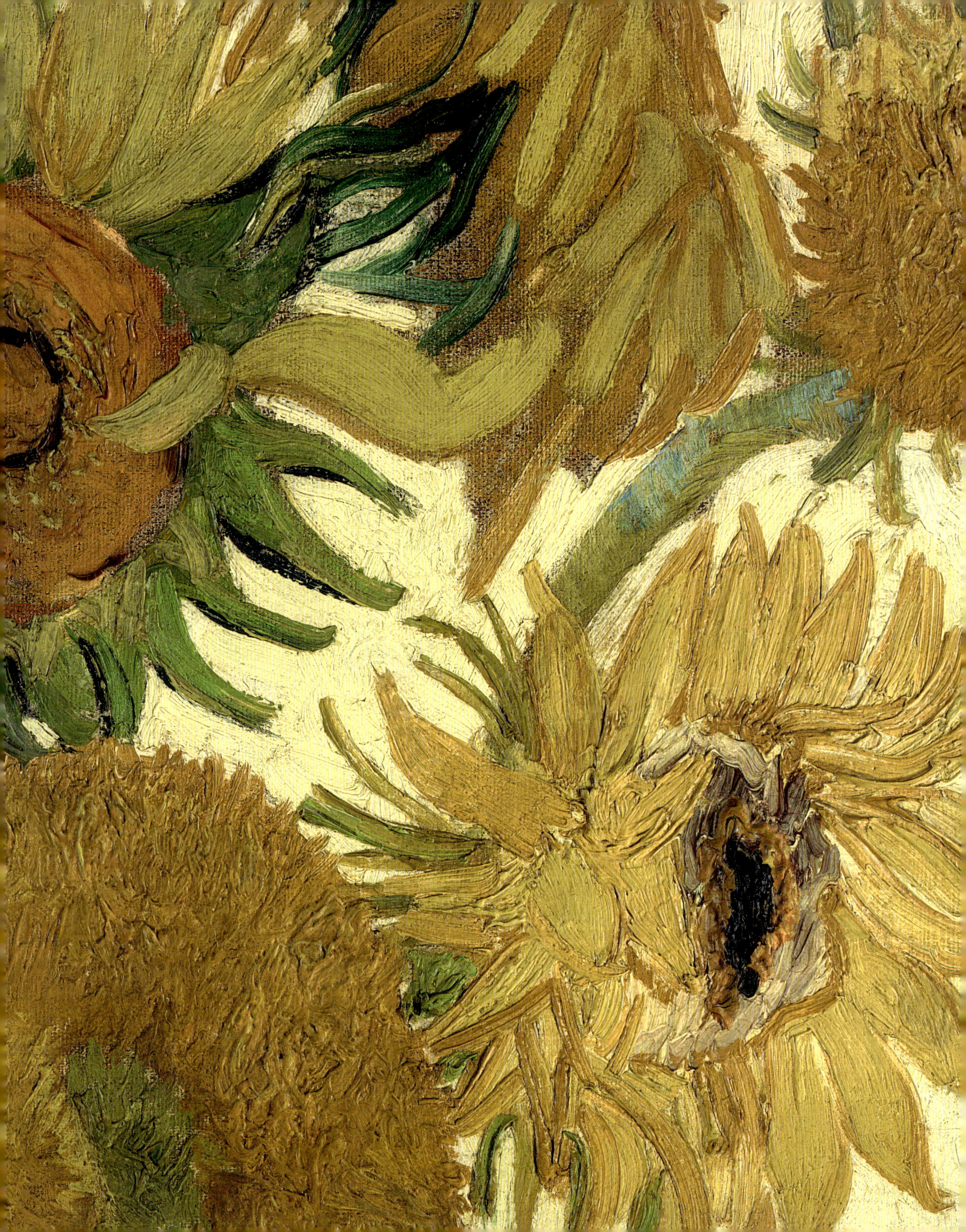

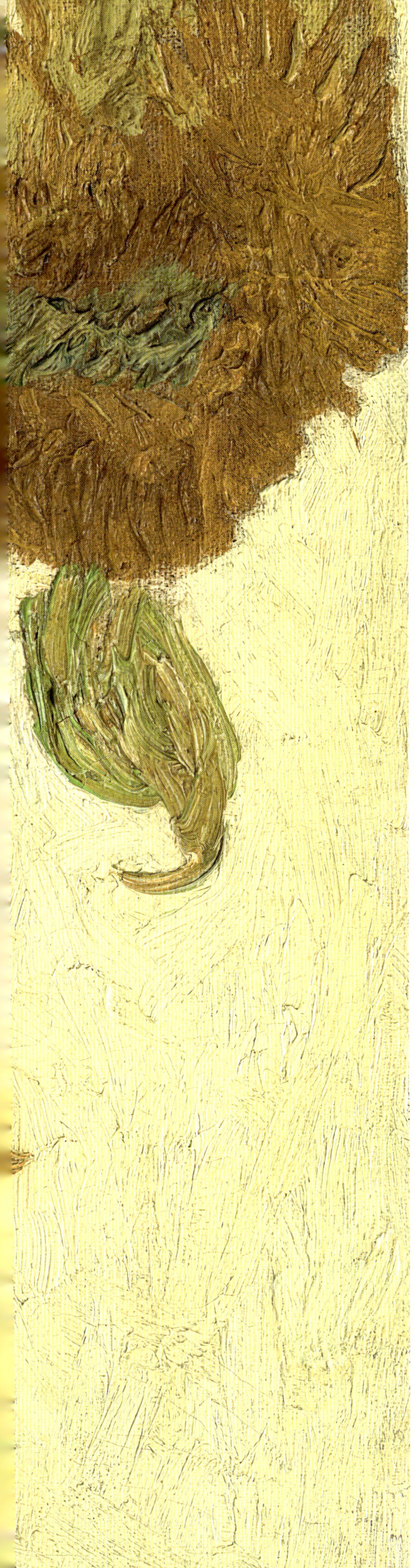

lines and unmodulated planes of color. Like Gauguin's puppies, they aim to capture the idea of a flower more than a copy after nature—the same ambition Gauguin held for his paintings from memory. While at work on the London canvas, Van Gogh expressed a version of this concept to his brother:

> This one creates quite an unusual effect, and I believe that this time it's painted with more simplicity than the quinces and lemons. Do you remember that one day at the Hôtel Drouot we saw a quite extraordinary Manet, some large pink peonies and their green leaves on a light background? As much in harmony and as much a *flower* as anything you like, and yet painted in solid, thick impasto . . .
>
> That's what I'd call simplicity of technique.[28]

Van Gogh's notion of "simplicity" resonates with Gauguin's theories of abstraction. In a letter to Bernard penned just weeks before Gauguin's arrival in Arles, Van Gogh offered a glimpse into the balance he sought between Bernard's and Gauguin's theories and his own practice. After insisting, "I never work from memory," he continued, "I can't work without a model. I'm not saying that I don't flatly turn my back on reality to turn a study into a painting—by arranging the colour, by enlarging, by simplifying—but I have such a fear of separating myself from what's possible and what's right as far as form is concerned."[29] By using a double negative, he revealed that he did indeed "turn [his] back on reality," recalling Gauguin's metaphorical "dreaming before nature." The way in which he did this—"by arranging the colour, by enlarging, by simplifying"—parallels the aesthetic evolution of the sunflower series.

The Studio of the South

Van Gogh knew that his London and Munich sunflower paintings were a tremendous achievement, and when Gauguin saw them he, too, understood as much. Regarding these canvases, Van Gogh wrote that Gauguin stammered, "That— . . . that's . . . the flower."[30] Gauguin was stunned by his colleague's success. The sunflowers attained precisely what Gauguin sought in painting from memory: the idea of a higher form, the Ideal.[31] Yet Van Gogh had spent months writing of his resistance to painting from memory in his letters to Gauguin and Bernard.

Still life appears to have created an unspoken tension between Van Gogh and Gauguin at the start of their two months together in Arles—a period that would prove to be the only realization of Van Gogh's dream of the Studio of the South. That fall they ventured out into Arles together, painting the same landscapes, the same models, and the same cafés. It would have been easy to set up an arrangement of objects on a rainy day and paint the same still life, but they never went head-to-head in this genre. For nearly a month, neither artist painted a still life.

By mid-November, Van Gogh had grown increasingly receptive to the idea of painting from memory. While this approach may have remained rooted in practicality, as it offered a way to stay productive on rainy days,[32] he noted its impact on his work: "Gauguin gives me courage to imagine, and the things of the imagination do indeed take on a more mysterious character."[33] Around November 19, 1888, Van Gogh wrote to Theo, "Gauguin, in spite of himself and in spite of me, has proved to me a little that it was time for me to vary things a bit—I'm beginning to compose from memory."[34]

Homage in Still Life

Van Gogh and Gauguin each returned to painting still lifes around the same time as Van Gogh's announcement to Theo that he was beginning to work from memory. In the same letter, he described to Theo two new paintings of chairs, now known as *Van Gogh's Chair* and *Gauguin's Chair* (*figs. 17, 18*). Each of these chairs is a stand-in for a portrait of the "sitter" named in the pictures' respective titles. The humble wicker

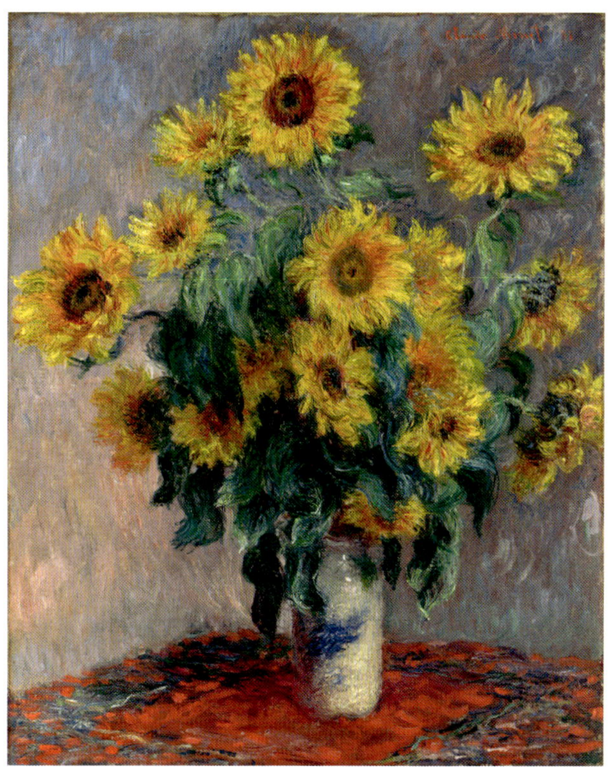

Fig. 16
Claude Monet (French, 1840–1926)
Bouquet of Sunflowers
1881
Oil on canvas
39¾ × 32 in. (101 × 81 cm)
The Metropolitan Museum of Art, New York: H. O. Havemeyer Collection, Bequest of Mrs. H. O. Havemeyer, 1929, 29.100.107

chair with a pipe and tobacco represents Van Gogh, and the floodlit composition corresponds with his preference for painting from nature. For Gauguin's chair, Van Gogh associated nighttime with imagination, so the picture's nocturnal setting evokes Gauguin's preferred method of working from memory.[35] In this way, the chairs are themselves metaphors for the process of painting from memory versus from nature.

Gauguin started upon a still life of his own within days of Van Gogh beginning the chair paintings. Van Gogh described Gauguin's canvas as "a big still life of an orange pumpkin and some apples and white linen on a yellow background and foreground"; in a letter sent just over one week later, he noted how much he liked the painting.[36] Gauguin admired Van Gogh's yellow-on-yellow compositions, particularly his sunflowers set against a yellow wall (see pp. 10–11). He had recently complimented Van Gogh's *Sunflowers* by telling the Dutch artist that he preferred them to Claude Monet's painting of the same subject (*fig. 16*).[37] For Gauguin to undertake the same yellow color scheme—and in a still life no less—was a form of homage to his colleague. Gauguin's painting of a pumpkin and apples was long thought lost or destroyed, but it is now believed that the original canvas was cut down and survives as Gauguin's *Little Cat* (1888; *fig. 20*).[38]

Around this time, Van Gogh likely undertook a repetition of his yellow-on-yellow sunflower painting, which is now in Tokyo (see pp. 18–19). While this work's date is relatively challenging to pinpoint because it is not specifically mentioned in any of Van Gogh's letters, the painting is on the same type of jute canvas that Van Gogh and Gauguin were using at this time, including for *Little Cat* and the two portraits discussed below. They ran out of this material by the time Gauguin left Arles in late December 1888, leading scholars to conclude that Van Gogh must have undertaken the Tokyo *Sunflowers* before Gauguin's departure, and likely around December 1.[39] This means that Van Gogh revisited his yellow-on-yellow sunflower painting on the heels of Gauguin working on his own still life "on a yellow background and foreground."

In this spirit of mutual respect, each artist set to work on a portrait of the other in the act of painting a still life. Gauguin's portrait of his friend, *Vincent van Gogh Painting Sunflowers* (1888; *fig. 19*), alludes to Van Gogh's sunflower

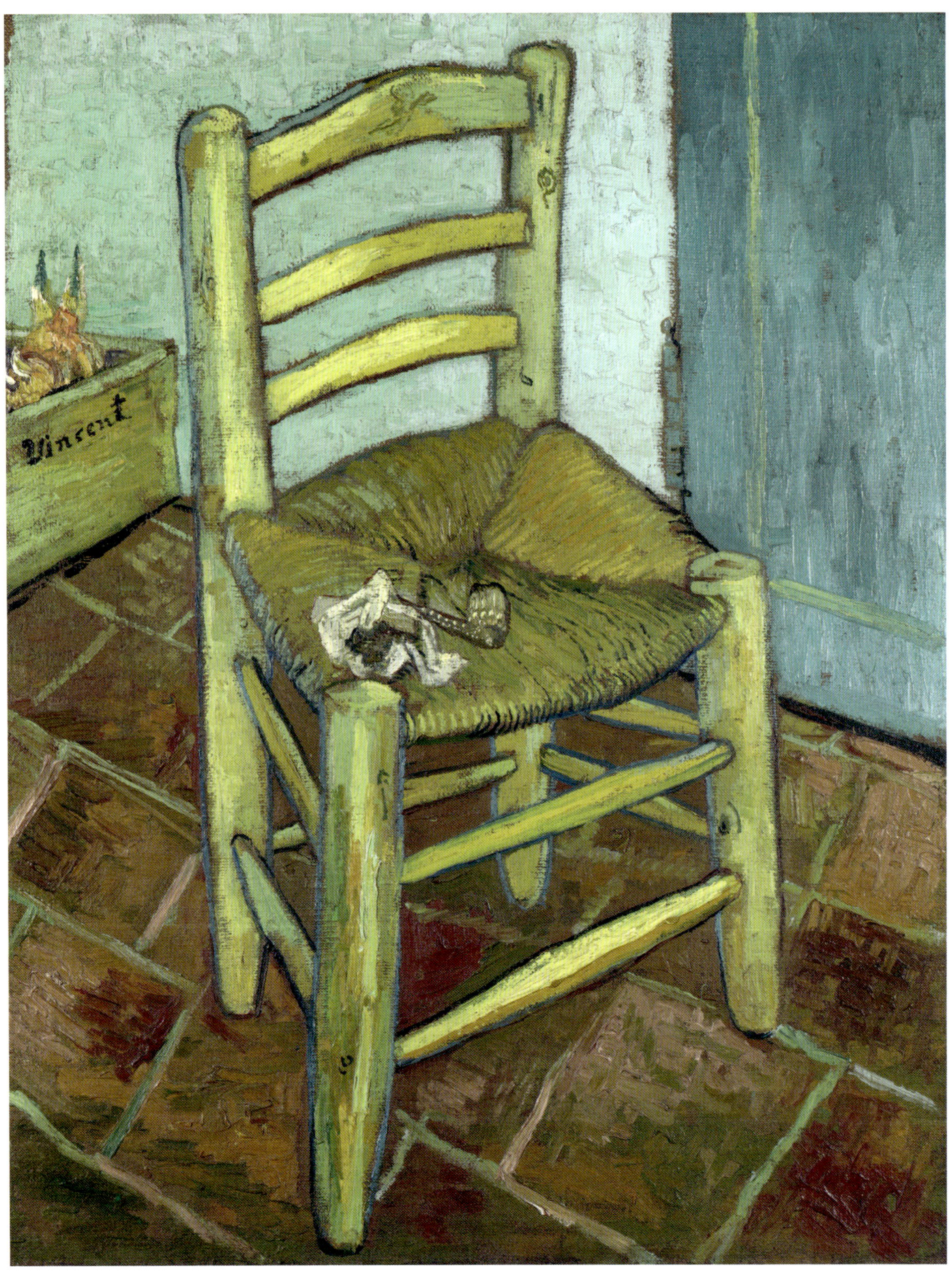

Fig. 17
Vincent van Gogh (Dutch, 1853–1890)
Van Gogh's Chair
Arles, November 1888
Oil on canvas
36⅛ × 28¾ in. (91.8 × 73 cm)
The National Gallery, London:
Bought, Courtauld Fund, 1924, NG3862

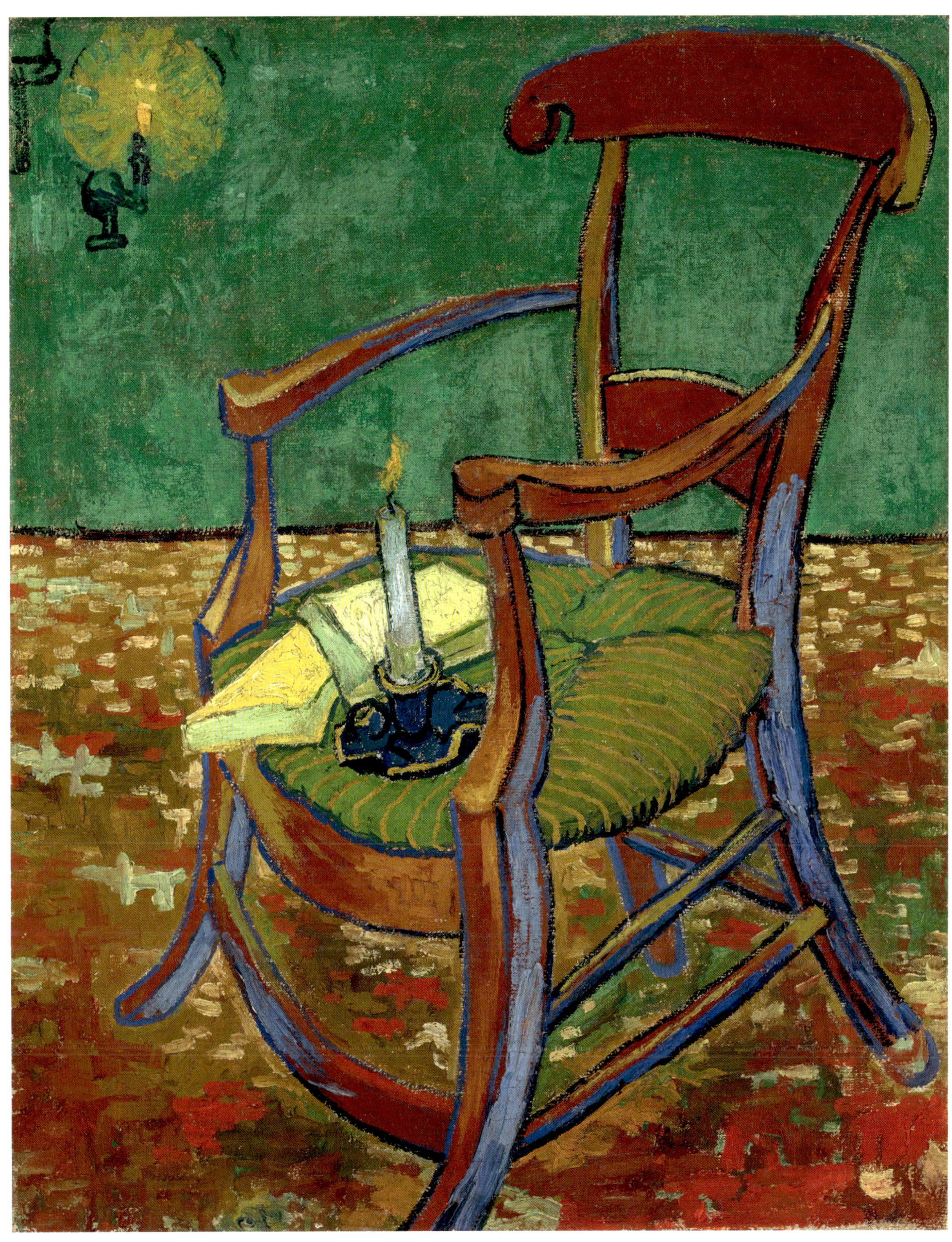

Fig. 18
Vincent van Gogh
Gauguin's Chair
Arles, November 1888
Oil on canvas
35⅝ × 28⅝ in. (90.5 × 72.7 cm)
Van Gogh Museum, Amsterdam
(Vincent van Gogh Foundation)

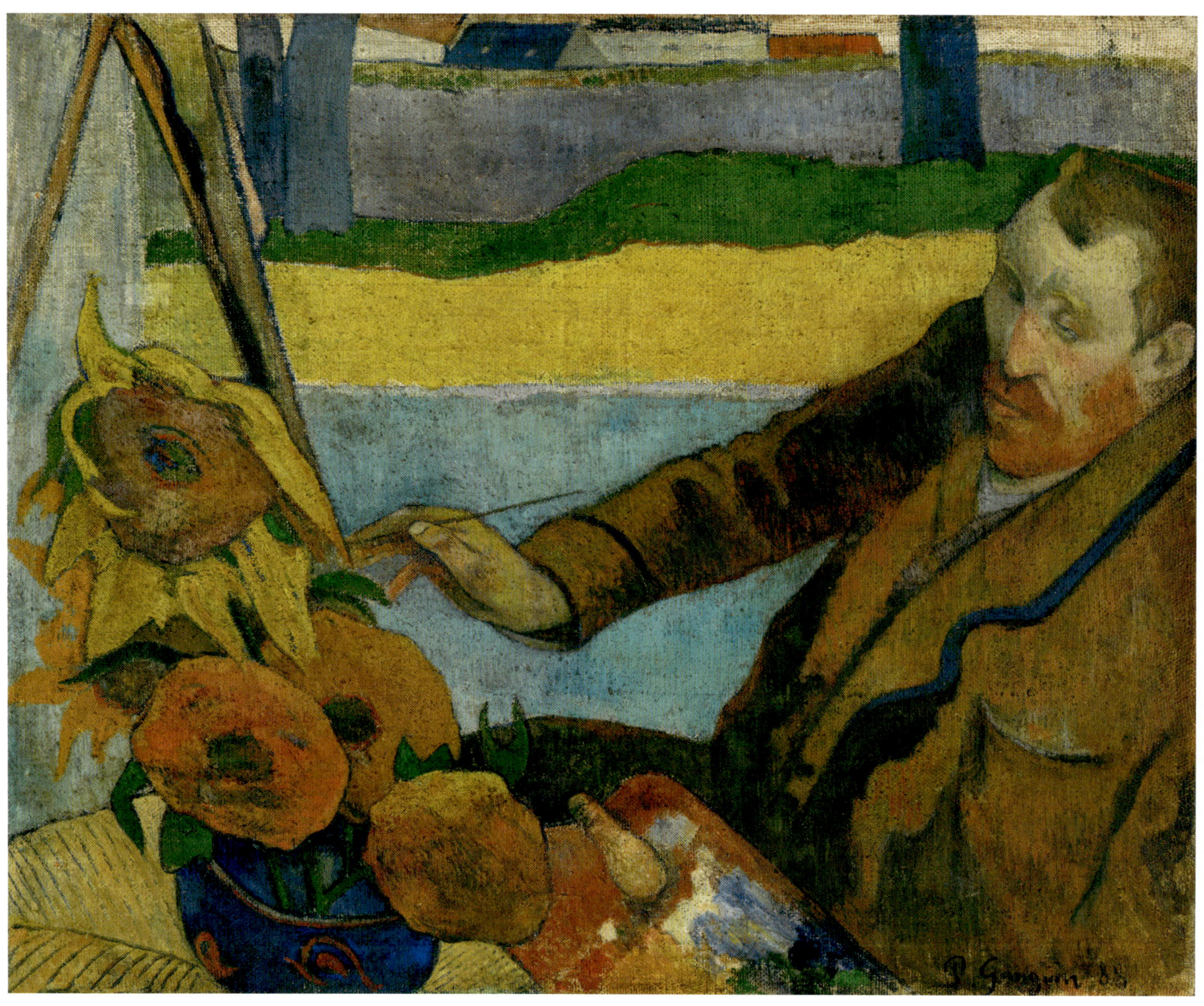

canvases and to *Van Gogh's Chair*, recalled in Gauguin's picture by the wicker chair atop which the flowers sit. In Van Gogh's painting of Gauguin (*fig. 21*), the canvas shown on the artist's easel is widely believed to represent the still life of a pumpkin and apples that now survives as *Little Cat*; indeed, in the letter in which Van Gogh praised that work, he announced that Gauguin had begun his portrait.[40] Continuing this reciprocity, Van Gogh painted Gauguin's portrait in a style that is highly evocative of that of his sitter. For example, the expansive, unmodulated planes of bright color that Van Gogh painted up to the contour lines but not over them are characteristic of Gauguin's work but relatively unusual for Van Gogh.

Fig. 19
Paul Gauguin
Vincent van Gogh Painting Sunflowers
Arles, December 1888
Oil on canvas
28¾ × 35$^{13}/_{16}$ in. (73 × 91 cm)
Van Gogh Museum, Amsterdam
(Vincent van Gogh Foundation)

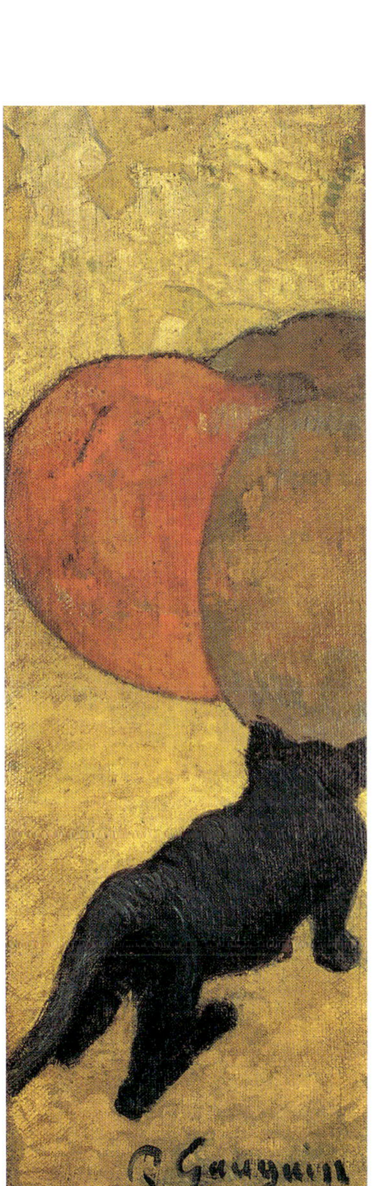

Fig. 20
Paul Gauguin
Little Cat
Arles, November 1888
Oil on canvas
$28\frac{3}{8} \times 9\frac{7}{16}$ in. (72 × 24 cm)
Private collection

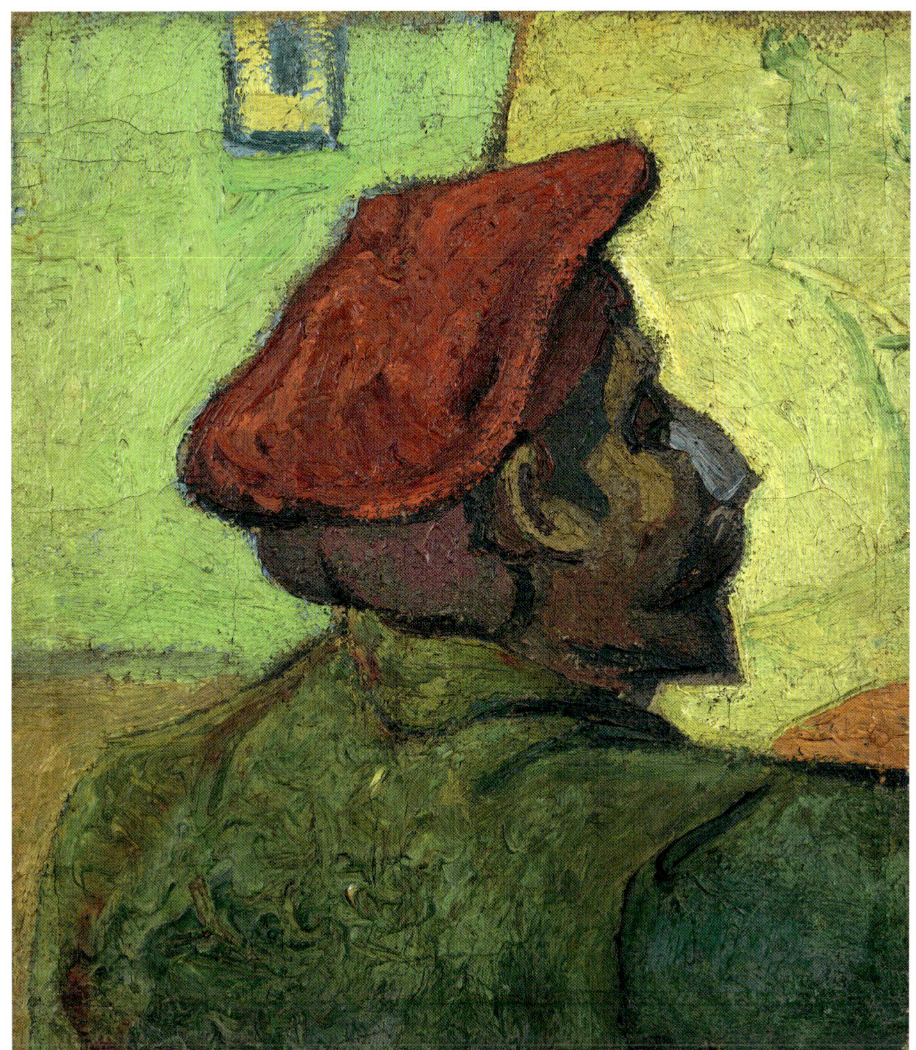

Fig. 21
Vincent van Gogh
Portrait of Gauguin
Arles, December 1888
Oil on jute on panel
$14\frac{15}{16} \times 13\frac{3}{8}$ in. (38 × 34 cm)
Van Gogh Museum, Amsterdam
(Vincent van Gogh Foundation)

The Painter of Sunflowers

Gauguin is said to have been the first admirer of Van Gogh's *Sunflowers*, and along with the many quotations and letters that bear this out,[41] his portrait of Van Gogh at work is perhaps our best evidence of the profound regard he held for those paintings. The portrait has elicited a range of interpretations concerning the nature of the portrayal, from derogatory to reverential or multivalent. All agree that the painting engages with the debate over working from memory.[42] In a preparatory sketch, Gauguin gave his sitter simian facial features, as if Van Gogh mindlessly "aped" nature by copying it directly onto his canvas (*fig. 22*). But the painting's relationship with the question of copying from nature versus composing from the imagination is more complex than the sketch would suggest. For one, Gauguin could not have witnessed Van Gogh painting a bouquet of fresh sunflowers because they would not have been available in December, when he painted this portrait. While Van Gogh likely did paint sunflowers that December, he used his canvases completed in August as models. Therefore, both Van Gogh and Gauguin worked not from nature but from Van Gogh's painted representation of it, redoubling the creative role of the artist's imagination.[43]

The sunflowers themselves add to the imagined rather than observed quality of this portrait. The uppermost flower reveals an eye and eyebrow that give it an eerie anthropomorphism. The vase is a low and wide vessel, and the flower stems, instead of resting on the container's edge, stand up independently of the rim, floating of their own accord. The faces of the five flowers turn not toward Van Gogh, who would presumably wish to see them, but to the viewer, pointing all the more to the invented nature of this scene.

Gauguin's representation of Van Gogh provides further insight into Gauguin's commentary on his colleague and their respective theories of painting from memory. From a distance, Van Gogh's eyes appear closed, but upon closer inspection, we see that they are half-closed. While this can be read negatively, in the sense that he is squinting or straining to observe the details of nature, an alternative view holds that his eyes are half-closed to blur and abstract his subject, to turn inward and work from the imagination. This is in

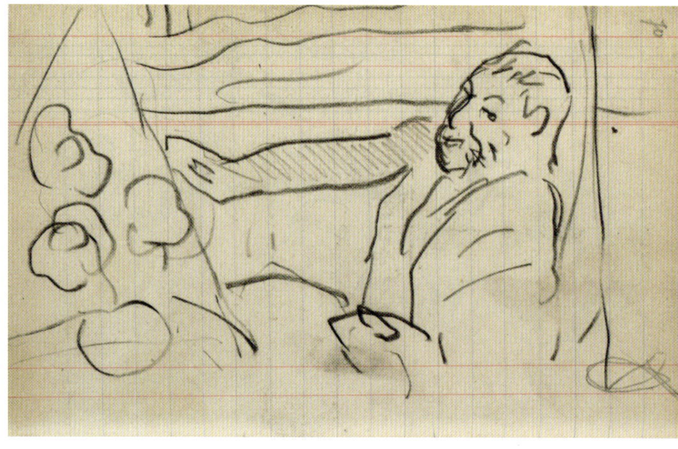

Fig. 22
Paul Gauguin
Study for *Vincent van Gogh Painting Sunflowers*
Page from the Carnet Huyghe, Arles, December 1888
Graphite and charcoal on lined ledger paper
4⅛ × 6¹¹⁄₁₆ in. (10.5 × 17 cm)
The Israel Museum, Jerusalem: Gift of Mr. Sam Salz, New York, through America-Israel Cultural Foundation, B72.0043/70-71

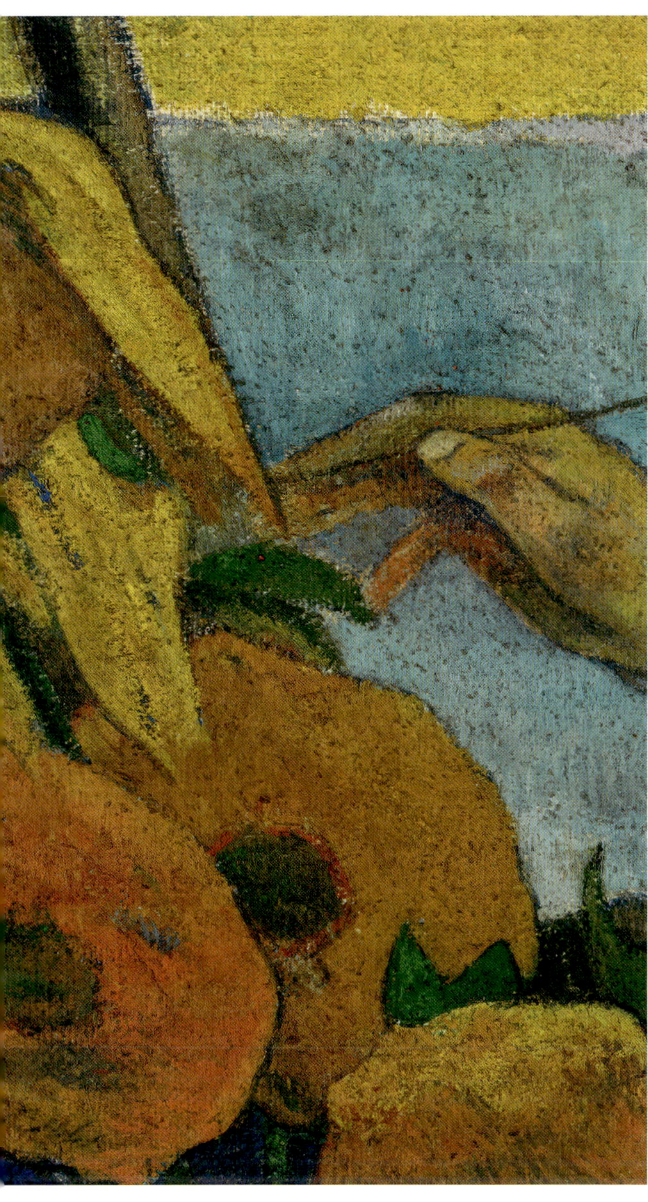

Fig. 23
Paul Gauguin
Vincent van Gogh Painting Sunflowers
(detail of fig. 19)

keeping with a notion that Gauguin quoted in a manuscript: "We can always double the beauty of a landscape by looking at it with eyes half-closed."[44] In the preparatory sketch, Van Gogh's left eye is open, looking brazenly at the viewer, as he sits with rolled-back shoulders and a rigid outstretched right arm. In the painting, Van Gogh's left eye looks down toward the sunflowers. Gauguin reined in the simian quality of the face and the bravura suggested in the drawing. Van Gogh instead appears more pensive in the painting, as if he is lost in thought.

A painted representation of a palette has long served as a metaphor for the creative process. The colors on Van Gogh's palette would most logically represent the colors he places on his canvas; but what, then, is the role of the light blue? While the vase is dark blue, the lighter color does not exist in the model Van Gogh observes. One possibility is that Van Gogh is painting a blue background for his sunflowers, which would match one of the two versions that was hanging in Gauguin's room at the time (see pp. 14–15), but the sunflowers Van Gogh was painting at this moment were on a yellow background. More wittily, the palette we see may be Gauguin's, as the colors depicted are the same colors he used throughout this canvas, including the swath of light blue for the wall. This intensifies the question that animates the composition—what is real or observed, and what exists only in the artist's imagination?

The depiction of Van Gogh's canvas raises the same question. The single line that designates the canvas merges with the gently curving edge of the flower petal, as if the petal remains to be painted (*fig. 23*).[45] At the tip of the petal, the painted canvas ends as well. Upon closer inspection, Van Gogh's fingers appear behind the line of the canvas or petal. For his fingers to appear behind the canvas-turned-petal suggests that it is not the canvas that his fingers touch, but the petal. His pinkie finger makes contact with the green leaf of the flower.[46] At the same time, the brush merges with the blue-gray shadows between his fingers, becoming so thin that it dissolves. All that remains are his three fingers, which touch, or even hold, the flower's petal. The foreshortening of his arm implies that he is reaching across his body and toward the picture plane, to the flowers rather than the canvas. Gauguin's emphatic attention to fingers and touch highlights the simultaneous materiality and immateriality of the sunflowers. The preexistence of the model, or of nature, is called into question in the act of creating the sunflowers before the viewer's eyes. Indeed, the tips of the lower-right petals on the same sunflower are also incomplete, as if Van Gogh has yet to paint them. With this composition, Gauguin pictured Van Gogh, eyes half-closed, conjuring a still life from within himself. He is not painting his canvas but inventing the model.

Gauguin thereby placed Van Gogh and his sunflowers at the center of a sophisticated treatise on painting from memory, the imagination, and the creative process. This portrait gives form to Gauguin's theory of painting from memory that derives from Baudelaire, wherein nature is a human construct and therefore cannot be copied until it is first imagined.[47] Reality derives from imagination. In the same way, Gauguin calls into question the existence of the sunflowers—of the model, of nature—prior to Van Gogh's creative act.

Nearly a year later, Van Gogh wrote to Theo of the portrait, "It was indeed me, extremely tired and charged with electricity as I was then."[48] The two artists' stay together in the small Yellow House had come to an abrupt end in late December 1888, when Van Gogh suffered a mental breakdown and sliced off part of his left ear. The police found him the following morning and brought him to the hospital, and Gauguin alerted Theo, who arrived in Arles the following day. After Theo ensured his brother was settled in the hospital, he and Gauguin left for Paris.

Remembering the Studio of the South

Despite the unsettling end to Van Gogh and Gauguin's time together in Arles, in the following months each artist continued to recall the other through still life. In January 1889, Gauguin visited Theo at his home in Paris and saw Van Gogh's yellow still life of quinces painted over a year earlier (see *fig. 27*), which Van Gogh had compared to his sunflower paintings while they were underway in August 1888.[49] Gauguin remarked upon it favorably to Van Gogh, and in the same letter, he asked for one of Van Gogh's

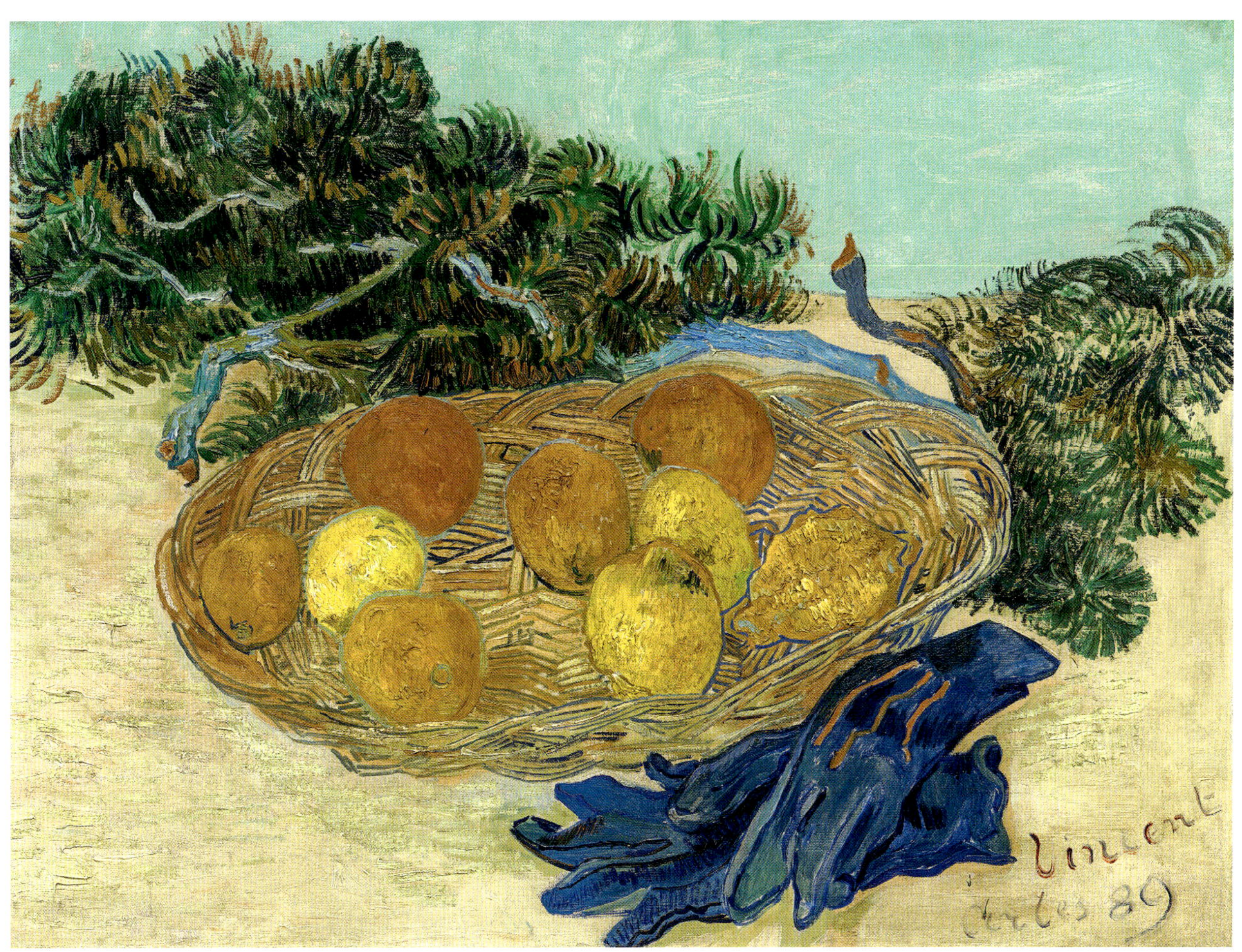

Fig. 24
Vincent van Gogh
Still Life of Oranges and Lemons with Blue Gloves
Arles, January 1889
Oil on canvas
18 7/8 × 24 7/16 in. (48 × 62 cm)
National Gallery of Art, Washington, DC: Collection of Mr. and Mrs. Paul Mellon, 2014.18.13

sunflower paintings, the version now in London (see pp. 10–11), in exchange for a few studies he had left in Arles.[50] Given the circumstances surrounding Gauguin's departure from Arles, Van Gogh took affront to this shameless and significant request. He had no intention of obliging at first, and took some time before responding.[51] During that period of reflection, Van Gogh painted *Still Life of Oranges and Lemons with Blue Gloves* (1889; *fig. 24*).[52] This composition bears distinct traces of Gauguin's influence, particularly in Van Gogh's use of blue contour lines around the fruit and gloves, the relatively flat planes of color, and the way the fruit seems to float in the basket independent of gravity—a favored still-life trick of Gauguin's. Within a day of reporting to Theo that he had completed this painting, Van Gogh replied to Gauguin's request for his London *Sunflowers*: "It's my intention, after what has happened, to contest categorically your right to the canvas in question. But as I commend your intelligence in the choice of that canvas I'll make an effort to paint two of them, exactly the same."[53]

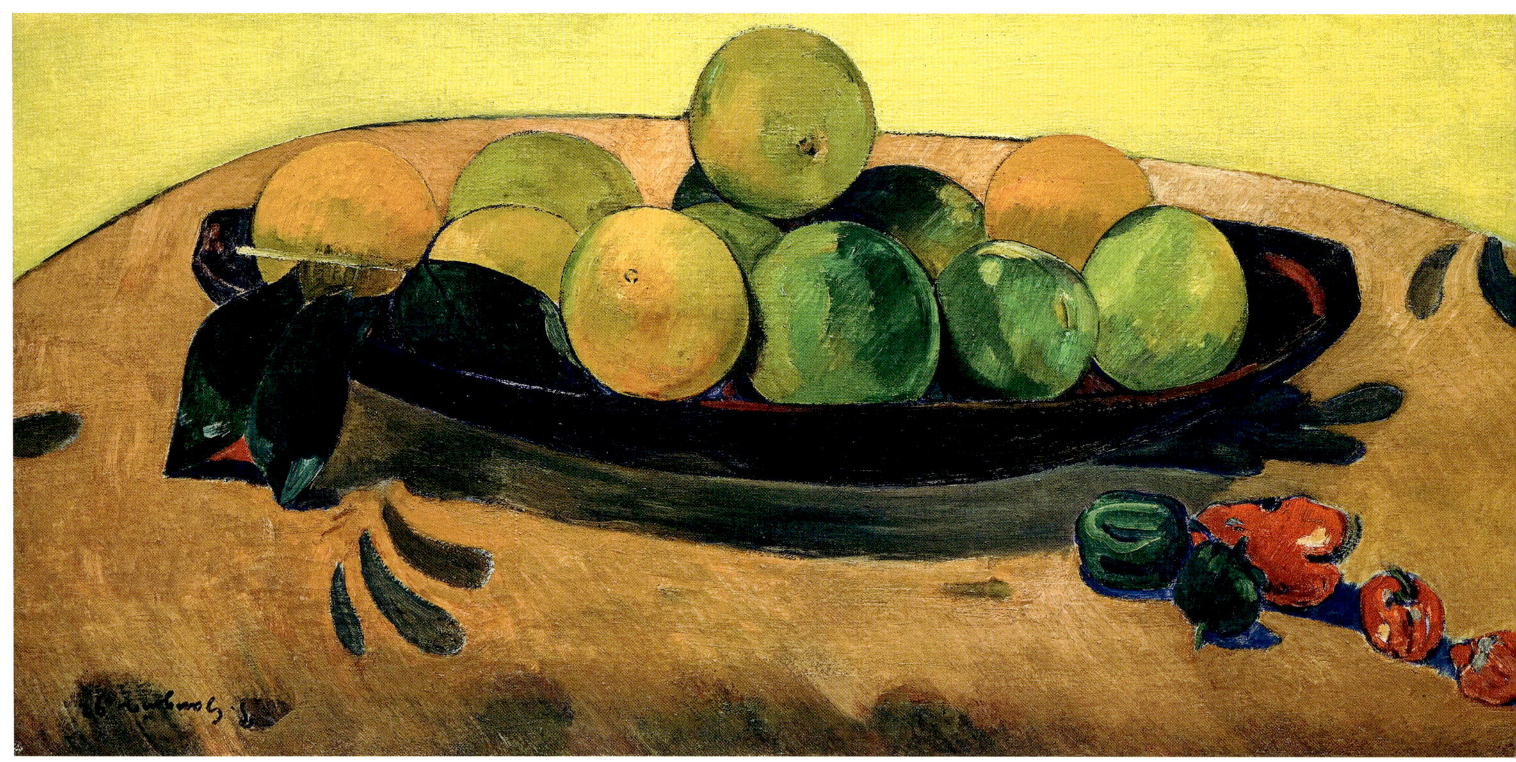

Fig. 25
Paul Gauguin
Still Life with Oranges and Peppers
1892
Oil on canvas
12½ × 26 in. (31.7 × 66 cm)
Private collection

Within seven days, Van Gogh created two additional sunflower paintings (see pp. 22–23, 26–27) that are as ambitious, imaginative, and monumental as the August paintings (see pp. 10–11, 14–15).[54] While they are remarkably similar to their August counterparts, they also bear notable differences in their aesthetic. In comparing the London painting to its repetition in Amsterdam, for example, we see that in the later version the petals are flatter and less modeled, the contour lines around the flower petals are even bolder, the yellows more brilliant, and the blue center of the flower on the right divorced entirely from reality. Van Gogh painted these canvases not from "nature" but from his own artworks. Akin to Gauguin painting Van Gogh's portrait as the painter of sunflowers, in keeping with Baudelaire, these flowers exist because Van Gogh had first imagined them. And from his imagination, he abstracted them further: The January canvases, even more so than the August canvases, are the "idea" of the flower.

With the tragic death of Van Gogh in July 1890, Gauguin lost his friend, creative competitor, and thought partner. For the rest of his life, Gauguin would return repeatedly to Van Gogh's *Sunflowers*, and through them he kept their dialogue alive. Following Gauguin's arrival in

Tahiti a year after Van Gogh's death, he revisited the idea of the yellow-on-yellow still-life composition, this time featuring a bowl of Tahitian oranges (*fig. 25*). Echoing the sunflowers, the yellow of the oranges appears against a wall and a table of the same color. Like Van Gogh's sunflower vases that appear to divert the line of the table downward, Gauguin's table seems to curve upward, around the uppermost orange. Defying gravity and awash in an otherworldly color, the tableau is insistently imaginative and surely painted from memory. The oranges share with religious icons a golden tone and stark simplicity, echoing the spiritual quality Van Gogh had come to find in his sunflowers. Like an altar to Van Gogh, the oranges are treated as objects of reverence and remembrance.

Untethered from trompe l'oeil and united with the process of painting from memory, still life raised for these artists new questions about abstraction and the meaning of representation. Each artist aimed to touch the soul—to move their viewers through color and composition—and they understood memory and imagination as the vehicle to do so. While this concept is an ancient one, for two months in the Yellow House in 1888, Van Gogh and Gauguin's impassioned and generative struggle opened new avenues to explore the realm of the imagination and to liberate the creative process, for themselves and for generations of artists to come.

This essay is developed from my doctoral dissertation, "Objects of Memory: Paul Gauguin and Still-Life Painting, 1880–1901" (University of Maryland, 2017). My adviser, June Hargrove, through her work on Gauguin, provided foundational inspiration for mine. I am ever grateful for her advice and continued support.

1. Vincent van Gogh to Theo van Gogh, Arles, December 17 or 18, 1888, in *Vincent van Gogh: The Letters*, ed. Leo Jansen, Hans Luijten, and Nienke Bakker (Van Gogh Museum & Huygens ING, 2009), online version December 2024, letter 726, https://vangoghletters.org. All correspondence to or from Van Gogh cited herein is from this source. Formatting from Van Gogh's original letters, including emphasized words and line and paragraph breaks, has been retained. This essay's opening quotation is from Vincent van Gogh to Theo van Gogh, Arles, on or about November 19, 1888, letter 721.
2. Van Gogh referred to his home and studio in Arles as the "little yellow house" at least seven times in letters written between June 1888 and February 1889. The first mention was in a letter to his sister: Vincent van Gogh to Willemien van Gogh, Arles, between June 16 and 20, 1888, letter 626. The "Studio of the South" is not a direct quotation of Van Gogh's but refers to his desire to establish an artists' colony in a warm and sunny place, not necessarily confined to France. Even while living in Arles, he continued to refine this dream and described the idea as "un atelier dans le midi" (a studio in the South) in letters to his brother. See Vincent van Gogh to Theo van Gogh, Arles, September 4, 1888, letter 674; and Arles, October 10 or 11, 1888, letter 702.
3. "Paints from the imagination"; Vincent van Gogh to Émile Bernard, Arles, July 29, 1888, letter 649. For "with eyes half-closed," see note 44 in the present essay; for "dreaming before [nature]," see note 6 in the present essay. Van Gogh described painting or working *de tête* on at least nine occasions in 1888 alone. See Van Gogh to Bernard, Arles, July 29, 1888, letter 649; and Arles, on or about October 5, 1888, letter 698; and Vincent van Gogh to Theo van Gogh, Arles, September 23 or 24, 1888, letter 686; Arles, September 25, 1888, letter 687; Arles, September 29, 1888, letter 691; Arles, October 9 or 10, 1888, letter 700; Arles, on or about November 3, 1888, letter 717; Arles, November 10, 1888, letter 718; and Arles, on or about November 19, 1888, letter 721. For a specific mention of working "from memory" (*de mémoire*), see, for example, Paul Gauguin to Vincent van Gogh, Pont-Aven, on or about September 26, 1888, letter 688.
4. Yadin Dudai and Mary Carruthers, "The Janus Face of Mnemosyne," *Nature* 434 (March 31, 2005): 567.
5. Paul Gauguin to Émile Schuffenecker, January 14, 1885, in Paul Gauguin, *The Writings of a Savage*, ed. Daniel Guérin, trans. Eleanor Levieux (Viking, 1978), 5; for the original letter, see *Correspondance de Paul Gauguin: Documents, témoignages*, ed. Victor Merlhès (Fondation Singer-Polignac, 1984), 1:89.
6. "Un conseil, ne copiez pas trop d'après la nature. L'art est une abstraction, tirez-la de la nature en rêvant devant et pensez plus à la création qu'au résultat." Gauguin to Schuffenecker, August 14, 1888, in Gauguin, *Correspondance*, 1:210 (except as noted, translations are my own).
7. "Forme de transition entre la représentation et le pur concept, que l'on désigne actuellement sous le nom d'image générique"; Théodule Armand Ribot, *Essai sur l'imagination créatrice* (F. Alcan, 1900), 16.
8. For example, Van Gogh specifically referenced the periodical in a letter to his brother; Vincent van Gogh to Theo van Gogh, Arles, September 23 or 24, 1888, letter 686. Jansen, Luijten, and Bakker (*Vincent van Gogh: The Letters*) have cited specific articles that appeared in the *Revue des deux mondes* as sources for ideas that Van Gogh expressed in his letters over a period ranging from 1876 to 1890; see their annotations in, among others, Vincent van Gogh to Theo van Gogh, Paris, July 15, 1875, letter 38, n3; and Van Gogh to Bernard, Arles, June 26, 1888, letter 632, n24. More broadly, Filiz Eda Burhan uncovered a vast trove of psychological and philosophical texts that had important ramifications for Gauguin and Symbolist theory; see Filiz Eda Burhan, "Vision and Visionaries: Nineteenth-Century Psychological Theory, the Occult Sciences, and the Formation of the Symbolist Aesthetic in France" (PhD diss., Princeton University, 1979). See also Dario Gamboni, *Paul Gauguin: The Mysterious Centre of Thought*, trans. Chris Miller (Reaktion Books, 2014), 52–54.
9. "Une idée générale et typique. La généralisation spontanée s'accomplit mécaniquement par la fusion des images dans la mémoire." Alfred Fouillée, "La survivance et la sélection des idées dans la mémoire," *Revue des deux mondes* 69, no. 5 (May 15, 1885): 365.
10. On Baudelaire's role in Gauguin's interest in correspondences of the senses, see Burhan, "Vision and Visionaries," 133–36; and June Hargrove, "Les *Contes barbares* de Paul Gauguin," *Revue de l'art*, no. 169 (2010): 26–28.
11. Robert L. Solso, *Cognition and the Visual Arts* (MIT Press, 1994), 236–37; and Stephen K. Reed, *Thinking Visually* (Psychology Press, 2010), 51–53.
12. Charles Baudelaire, *The Salon of 1846*, in *Baudelaire: Selected Writings on Art and Artists*, ed. and trans. P. E. Charvet (Cambridge University Press, 1981), 66–67; for the original, see Charles Baudelaire, *Salon de 1846*, in *Œuvres complètes de Charles Baudelaire* (Michel Lévy, 1868), 2:105.
13. Daniel Wildenstein, *Gauguin: A Savage in the Making; Catalogue Raisonné of the Paintings (1873–1888)* (Skira, 2002), 2:435; Béatrice Lovis, "Les natures mortes de Paul Gauguin: Une production picturale méconnue," *Artibus et historiae* 30, no. 59 (2009): 165; and Eliza E. Rathbone and George T. M. Shackelford, *Impressionist Still Life* (H. N. Abrams, 2001), 172.
14. Gauguin would have found confirmation of this intuition in the writings of Baudelaire and other nineteenth-century psychologists and philosophers who also wrote eloquently about contour and silhouette. More broadly, Vojtěch Jirat-Wasiutyński described *Still Life with Three Puppies* as Gauguin's first attempt to make a painting from memory; Vojtěch Jirat-Wasiutyński, *Paul Gauguin in the Context of Symbolism* (Garland, 1978), 92. The painting is dated to August 1888 in Wildenstein, *Gauguin*, 2:492.

15. Norman Bryson, *Looking at the Overlooked: Four Essays on Still-Life Painting* (Harvard University Press, 1990), 30–32; Meyer Schapiro, "The Apples of Cézanne: An Essay on the Meaning of Still Life" (1968), in *Modern Art: 19th & 20th Centuries; Selected Papers* (G. Braziller, 1979), 19–21; and S. Ebert-Schifferer, *Deceptions and Illusions: Five Centuries of Trompe l'Oeil Painting*, exh. cat. (National Gallery of Art, 2002).
16. See Paul Gauguin, *Diverses choses*, facsimile reproduction in *Gauguin écrivain: Ancien culte mahorie, Noa Noa, Diverses choses*, ed. Isabelle Cahn (Réunion des Musées Nationaux, 2003), 213, CD-ROM.
17. The centrality of the creative process for Gauguin and its link to his concept of artistic freedom derive from June Hargrove, notably her article "*Woman with a Fan*: Paul Gauguin's Heavenly Vairaumati; A Parable of Immortality," *Art Bulletin* 88, no. 3 (September 2006): 552–66.
18. This is an often-repeated point in still-life literature; see, for example, Schapiro, "Apples of Cézanne," 13.
19. See, for example, Vincent van Gogh to Theo van Gogh, Arles, July 8 or 9, 1888, letter 637; and Van Gogh to Bernard, Arles, on or about October 5, 1888, letter 698.
20. Vincent van Gogh to Theo van Gogh, Arles, September 23 or 24, 1888, letter 686.
21. Vincent van Gogh to Theo van Gogh, Nuenen, Netherlands, on or about April 28, 1885, letter 496. The original text is in Dutch. Note that Van Gogh used a Dutch phrase for painting from memory, *uit het hoofd*, which literally means "from the head" but is commonly translated, including by Jansen, Luijten, and Bakker in *Vincent van Gogh: The Letters*, as "from memory." (The same is true of the expression *de tête* in French, referenced in note 3 above.)
22. See Vincent van Gogh to Theo van Gogh, Nuenen, Netherlands, on or about April 28, 1885, letter 496, n6.
23. Van Gogh to Bernard, Arles, July 29, 1888, letter 649.
24. Gauguin to Van Gogh, Pont-Aven, on or about July 22, 1888, letter 646.
25. Gauguin to Van Gogh, Paris, December 1887, letter 576, n2.
26. See Van Gogh to Bernard, Arles, on or about August 21, 1888, letter 665; Vincent van Gogh to Theo van Gogh, Arles, August 21 or 22, 1888, letter 666; and Vincent van Gogh to Willemien van Gogh, Arles, August 21 or 22, 1888, letter 667.
27. Martin Bailey, *The Sunflowers Are Mine: The Story of Van Gogh's Masterpiece* (Frances Lincoln, 2013), 51.
28. Vincent van Gogh to Theo van Gogh, Arles, August 23 or 24, 1888, letter 668.
29. Van Gogh to Bernard, Arles, on or about October 5, 1888, letter 698.
30. "Cà— . . c'est . . la fleur"; Vincent van Gogh to Theo van Gogh, Arles, January 22, 1889, letter 741.
31. Douglas W. Druick and Peter Kort Zegers, *Van Gogh and Gauguin: The Studio of the South*, exh. cat. (Art Institute of Chicago, 2001), 240.
32. For example, "The weather's windy and rainy here, and I'm very happy not to be alone, I work from memory on bad days, and that wouldn't work if I were alone"; Vincent van Gogh to Theo van Gogh, Arles, November 10, 1888, letter 718.
33. Vincent van Gogh to Theo van Gogh, Arles, November 11 or 12, 1888, letter 719.
34. Vincent van Gogh to Theo van Gogh, Arles, on or about November 19, 1888, letter 721.
35. Petra Ten-Doesschate Chu, "Emblems for a Modern Age: Vincent van Gogh's Still Lifes and the Nineteenth-Century Vignette Tradition," in *The Object as Subject: Studies in the Interpretation of Still Life*, ed. Anne W. Lowenthal (Princeton University Press, 1996), 91–92, 97n34.
36. Vincent van Gogh to Theo van Gogh, Arles, on or about November 21, 1888, letter 722; and Arles, on or about December 1, 1888, letter 723.
37. According to Vincent van Gogh to Theo van Gogh, Arles, on or about November 19, 1888, letter 721.
38. Wildenstein, *Gauguin*, 2:533.
39. Druick and Zegers, *Van Gogh and Gauguin*, 240; Louis van Tilborgh and Ella Hendriks, "The Tokyo *Sunflowers*: A Genuine Repetition by Van Gogh or a Schuffenecker Forgery?," *Van Gogh Museum Journal*, 2001, p. 38, accessed October 18, 2025, https://www.dbnl.org/tekst/_van012200101_01/_van012200101_01_0003.php; Laura Coyle, "The Still-Life Paintings of Vincent van Gogh and Their Context" (PhD diss., Princeton University, 2007), 439–41; Gamboni, *Mysterious Centre of Thought*, 167; and Nienke Bakker and Christopher Riopelle, "The *Sunflowers* in Perspective," in *Van Gogh's Sunflowers Illuminated: Art Meets Science*, ed. Ella Hendriks and Marije Vellekoop (Amsterdam University Press, 2019), 31. These sources date the Tokyo painting to around December 1, 1888. Prior to 2001 it was dated to 1889, and at stake in the picture's dating is whether Gauguin observed Van Gogh painting sunflowers. Martin Bailey (*Sunflowers Are Mine*, 90–94) outlined reasons for and against an 1889 date based largely on the two artists' correspondence leading up to the creation of the sunflower paintings now in Philadelphia and Amsterdam (see pp. 22–23, 26–27) in January 1889.
40. Vincent van Gogh to Theo van Gogh, Arles, on or about December 1, 1888, letter 723. For the connection between Van Gogh's letter and the painting on Gauguin's easel in the portrait, see Martin Bailey, "Van Gogh's Portrait of Gauguin," *Apollo* 144, no. 413 (July 1996): 52; Druick and Zegers, *Van Gogh and Gauguin*, 236; and Vincent van Gogh to Theo van Gogh, Arles, on or about November 21, 1888, letter 722, n10.
41. See, for example, notes 30, 37, and 50 in the present essay; and note 33 in Thompson's essay in this volume.
42. See, for example, Vojtěch Jirat-Wasiutyński, "Painting from Nature Versus Painting from Memory," in *A Closer Look: Technical and Art-Historical Studies on Works by Van Gogh and Gauguin*, ed. Cornelia Peres, Michael Hoyle, and Louis van Tilborgh (Waanders, 1991), 95–101; Druick and Zegers, *Van Gogh and Gauguin*, 239–43; Coyle, "Still-Life Paintings," 442; and Gamboni, *Mysterious Centre of Thought*, 165–67. Druick and Zegers (*Van Gogh and Gauguin*, 243) note Gauguin's likely surprise at finding in Van Gogh an equal partner in their exchange of ideas, rather than the mentor-mentee relationship he had anticipated.
43. Druick and Zegers, *Van Gogh and Gauguin*, 240.
44. "Nous pouvons toujours doubler la beauté d'un paysage en le regardant les yeux à demi-clos"; this quotation appears under a section titled "Notes from Edgar Poe." Gauguin copied this passage from Edgar Allan Poe's *Marginalia*, which was translated into French and published as part of a compilation of abridged works by Poe in 1882. For a facsimile, see Paul Gauguin, *"À ma fille Aline, ce cahier est dédié": Notes éparses, sans suite comme les rêves, comme la vie toute fait de morceaux; Journal de jeune fille* (1893), ed. Victor Merlhès (William Blake, 1989), vol. 2, n.p. (p. 6 of the facsimile).
45. Gamboni, *Mysterious Centre of Thought*, 165; and Jirat-Wasiutyński, "Painting from Nature," 101.
46. This arrangement of fingers, with three straight and the pinkie bent, is rather awkward and suggests that the points of contact with the flower and leaf are deliberate. I am grateful to René Boitelle, senior paintings conservator at the Van Gogh Museum, for his analysis of the painting, which supports my interpretation that the placement of the fingers was purposeful and not a pentimento; René Boitelle, email message to the author, October 10, 2016.
47. Hans-Jost Frey, *Studies in Poetic Discourse: Mallarmé, Baudelaire, Rimbaud, Hölderlin* (Stanford University Press, 1996), 62–65, 72.
48. Vincent van Gogh to Theo van Gogh, Saint-Rémy-de-Provence, September 10, 1889, letter 801.
49. Gauguin mentioned visiting Theo in a letter to Vincent; see Gauguin to Van Gogh, Paris, between January 8 and 16, 1889, letter 734, n3, which identifies the painting as *Quinces, Lemons, Pears, and Grapes*. For Van Gogh's comparison of his London sunflower painting to this painting, see Vincent van Gogh to Theo van Gogh, Arles, on or about August 26, 1888, letter 669.
50. Gauguin to Van Gogh, Paris, between January 8 and 16, 1889, letter 734. On Gauguin's request for the sunflower painting, see letter 734 and n1 therein.
51. Vincent van Gogh to Theo van Gogh, Arles, January 17, 1889, letter 736.
52. Vincent van Gogh to Theo van Gogh, Arles, January 22, 1889, letter 741. Van Gogh reported he had finished the painting in this letter. The painting appears to have passages of wet-on-dry paint, suggesting he worked on it over a period of at least a few days.
53. Van Gogh to Gauguin, Arles, January 21, 1889, letter 739.
54. Vincent van Gogh to Theo van Gogh, Arles, January 28, 1889, letter 743.

“*No more than* I approve of its just lying about, *do I want* my work to be displayed in fluted frames in the leading galleries, you see.”

—Vincent van Gogh to Theo van Gogh
On or about March 2, 1884

Framing the Sunflowers

—*Tara Contractor*

Throughout his career, Vincent van Gogh thought carefully about how his paintings should be framed and displayed. This was especially true during the fifteen months, from February 1888 to May 1889, that he spent in Arles, the city in the South of France where he hoped to create the Studio of the South, a utopian community where like-minded artists could escape the pressures of urban life. Indeed, roughly half of his letters discussing frames come from this period.[1] As he produced paintings to fill the Yellow House, the two-bedroom home he had rented in Arles with hopes of establishing his community, he imagined frames with a renewed seriousness of purpose. His paintings of sunflowers, today some of his best-loved works, were at the heart of his experiments. While these paintings do not retain original frames, we can reconstruct what they may have looked like from surviving letters, paintings, and archival evidence. Close study of these absent frames reveals that as the sunflower paintings evolved, Van Gogh's ideas about framing and display became ever more intimately connected with his utopian ideals, with frames becoming mediums through which he contemplated his artistic practice and even purpose.

Van Gogh was working in a moment when artists were challenging traditional ideas about how paintings should be framed and displayed.[2] Following centuries of tradition, the French Salon, still the largest and most important exhibition venue in Europe, displayed paintings in densely hung groupings that spanned from chair rail to ceiling (*fig. 26*). Artists were required to surround their works in gilded frames, and they often chose wide, elaborately ornamented designs to attract attention. Revivalist styles, covered in the undulating flowers and acanthus leaves of eighteenth-century frames, were especially popular. From the mid-1850s, however, avant-garde artists in London and Paris began to experiment with simpler frames, which they treated as extensions of their artworks rather than mere display fittings. Artists such as James McNeill Whistler and Edgar Degas designed their own frames, sometimes even painting them with colors and patterns chosen to complement their canvases. In the 1880s, Neo-Impressionist painter Georges Seurat pushed these experiments further, occasionally surrounding his paintings with frames and borders that were, much like his pointillist canvases, densely covered in multicolored brushstrokes.[3] As artists embraced new ideas of "art for art's sake," relishing art for its visual pleasures rather than its narrative or moral purposes, exhibitions likewise became more attentive to crafting pleasurable, immersive viewing experiences.[4] Avant-garde artists pioneered new display practices, rejecting the Salon's densely hung walls for airier presentations with works exhibited in just one or two rows on carefully chosen wall colors.[5] Van Gogh's experiments with framing and display should be understood as efforts to participate in these trends.

Even in his early career, Van Gogh considered how frames might shift viewers' experiences of his art. Having worked for the art dealer and print publisher Goupil & Cie in its branches in The Hague, London, and Paris, he would have had firsthand experience with the way mats and frames can alter the appearances of prints and paintings.[6] He sought frames that set his work apart from the artistic mainstream, writing to his brother Theo in 1884, "I'm seeking something calm and something cool in my work. *No more than* I approve of its just lying about, *do I want* my work to be displayed in fluted frames in the leading galleries, you see."[7] Rejecting the fluted ornament of Salon frames, he distanced himself from the frenzied commercialism he associated with fashionable galleries.

Van Gogh was explicit about the types of frames he would have chosen instead: "I prefer to see my work in a deep black frame."[8] Given his financial constraints, it is unclear whether any of his works from this period were ever framed. Nevertheless, Van Gogh's stated preference for black frames makes visual sense, as they would have accentuated the subtle, almost somber palette of early works such as *Congregation Leaving the Reformed Church in Nuenen* (1884–85; Van Gogh Museum, Amsterdam). Black frames would have also conspicuously recalled the ebony frames used by seventeenth-century Dutch artists such as Rembrandt van Rijn, whose depictions of humble people and countryside views Van Gogh admired. Frames thus offered him a way to telegraph his inspirations and to stake a place in an art historical canon. Still, black was not the only finish he imagined for his frames in this period.

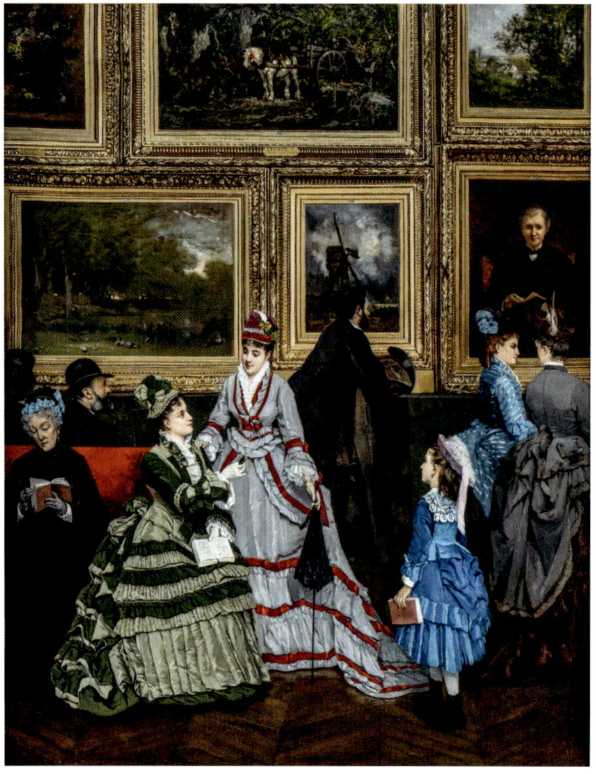

Fig. 26
Camille-Léopold Cabaillot-Lassalle (French, 1839–1902)
The Salon of 1874
1874
Oil on canvas
39⅜ × 32¹⁄₁₆ in. (100 × 81.5 cm)
Musée d'Orsay, Paris: Don de la Galerie Ary Jan et Segoura Fine Art, 2023

He wanted a gold frame for his first major painting, *The Potato Eaters* (1885; Van Gogh Museum, Amsterdam), which depicts a group of agricultural workers sitting down to enjoy their evening meal inside a shadowy cottage. A gold frame would have underscored the painting's references to contemporary Hague School artists, such as Jozef Israëls, who exhibited their scenes of humble rural life at the Salon to critical and commercial success. The gold frame planned for *The Potato Eaters* signaled Van Gogh's widening ambitions as well as his influences. Most importantly, however, a gold surround would have balanced the composition and completed its light and color effects. He explained that a gold frame or, barring that, a "wall hung with a paper that had a deep tone of ripe wheat" would replicate the effect of firelight on the cottage's walls, drawing out the blue tones in the shadows.[9] This attention to color contrasts was influenced by his study of Charles Blanc's *Grammaire des arts du dessin*, which disseminated French chemist Michel Eugène Chevreul's discovery that contrasting colors appear brighter in proximity to each other.[10] These joint concerns with color theory and art historical reference would continue to guide Van Gogh's ideas about framing and display in the years to come.

Only one of Van Gogh's original frames is known to have survived: that for *Quinces, Lemons, Pears, and Grapes* (1887; *fig. 27*). This painting is one of several still lifes that Van Gogh completed in Paris during the fall of 1887, but it stands out among these works for its almost monochromatic yellow palette and its frame enlivened with shimmering lemon-colored brushstrokes. With its simple profile and bold color, the frame likely reflects Van Gogh's awareness of colorful Impressionist and Neo-Impressionist frames.[11] It reads as an extension of the painting's surface, and thus relates closely to the painted borders he sometimes added to the edges of his works from 1885 on, such as the red border around his *Fishing in Spring, the Pont de Clichy (Asnières)* (1887; The Art Institute of Chicago).[12] Van Gogh's sense of the frame's importance to *Quinces, Lemons, Pears, and Grapes* is confirmed by the fact that he altered it as the canvas evolved. He eliminated a red line along the frame's inner edge and added the pattern of visible brushstrokes only *after* he painted the present still life over an earlier

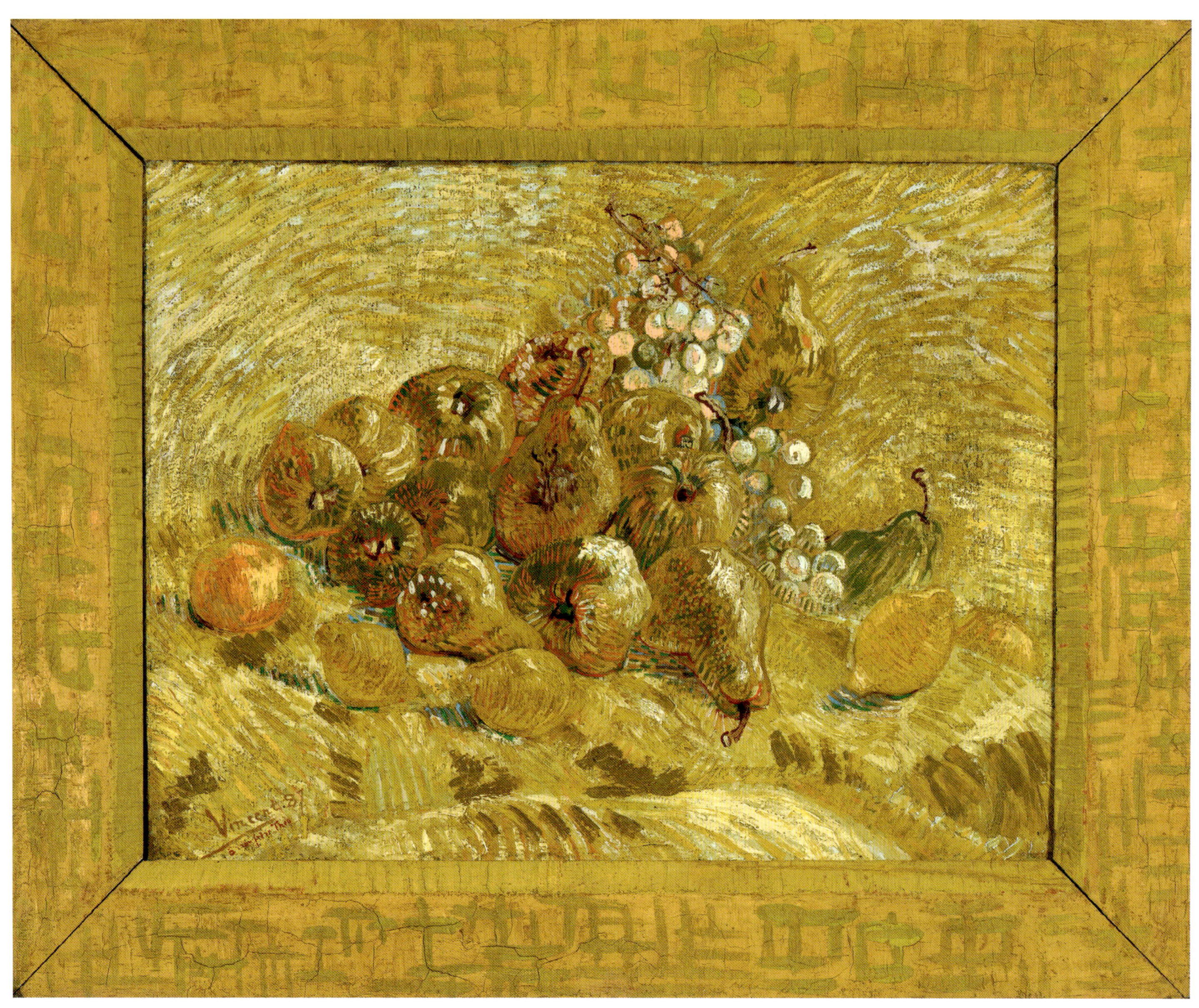

Fig. 27
Vincent van Gogh (Dutch, 1853–1890)
Quinces, Lemons, Pears, and Grapes
Paris, September–October 1887
Oil on canvas
19¼ × 25¹³⁄₁₆ in. (48.9 × 65.5 cm)
Framed: 26⁵⁄₁₆ × 32¹⁵⁄₁₆ in. (66.9 cm × 83.7 cm)
Van Gogh Museum, Amsterdam
(Vincent van Gogh Foundation)

landscape.[13] The visible brushstrokes remain the frame's most striking feature, immediately testifying to the care and attention he lavished upon it. As Van Gogh scholar Louis van Tilborgh has described, the grid-like pattern of these brushstrokes corresponds to the frame's rectangular shape and dynamically contrasts with the curved brushstrokes that articulate the contours of the fruits and draped fabric.[14] Extending the painting yet highlighting the geometry of a real surface, the frame's brushstrokes mediate between the spatial logic of the painting and the real world, embodying the sophistication of Van Gogh's framing experiments. Traces of colorful paint still visible on the edges of other canvases executed during his Paris period, from February 1886 to February 1888, suggest that they once had similar frames, likewise painted to complement and extend the compositions they enclosed.[15]

After Van Gogh arrived in Arles in February 1888, he continued to experiment with painted frames that echoed Impressionist styles, writing to Theo about his plans for frames in "cold white" and "warm cream."[16] These white frames likely resembled the wide white border in *Still Life with Coffeepot* (1888; *fig. 28*), which complements the picture's color harmonies by drawing out the creamy brightness of the porcelain even as a thinner red inner border accentuates the blues of the tablecloth and shadows. The scale of the white border in *Still Life with Coffeepot* recalls the frame surrounding *Quinces, Lemons, Pears, and Grapes*, and suggests the artist's continued preference for this wide, flat style. He may have imagined similar white frames for other still lifes painted around this time, such as the Barnes Foundation's *Still Life* (1888; *fig. 29*), which he likewise encircled with a thin red-orange border along three sides. As Barnes curator Cindy Kang has pointed out, the red stem lying near the picture's bottom edge playfully completes the three-sided border, a gesture that speaks to Van Gogh's continued interest in blurring the boundaries between paintings and frames.[17] He was also imagining idiosyncratic frame designs at this moment. In a letter describing *Bridge at Arles (Pont de Langlois)* (1888; Kröller-Müller Museum, Otterlo, Netherlands), for instance, he sketched a frame profile with a raised border on the outer edge, writing that this edge should be gold while the inner

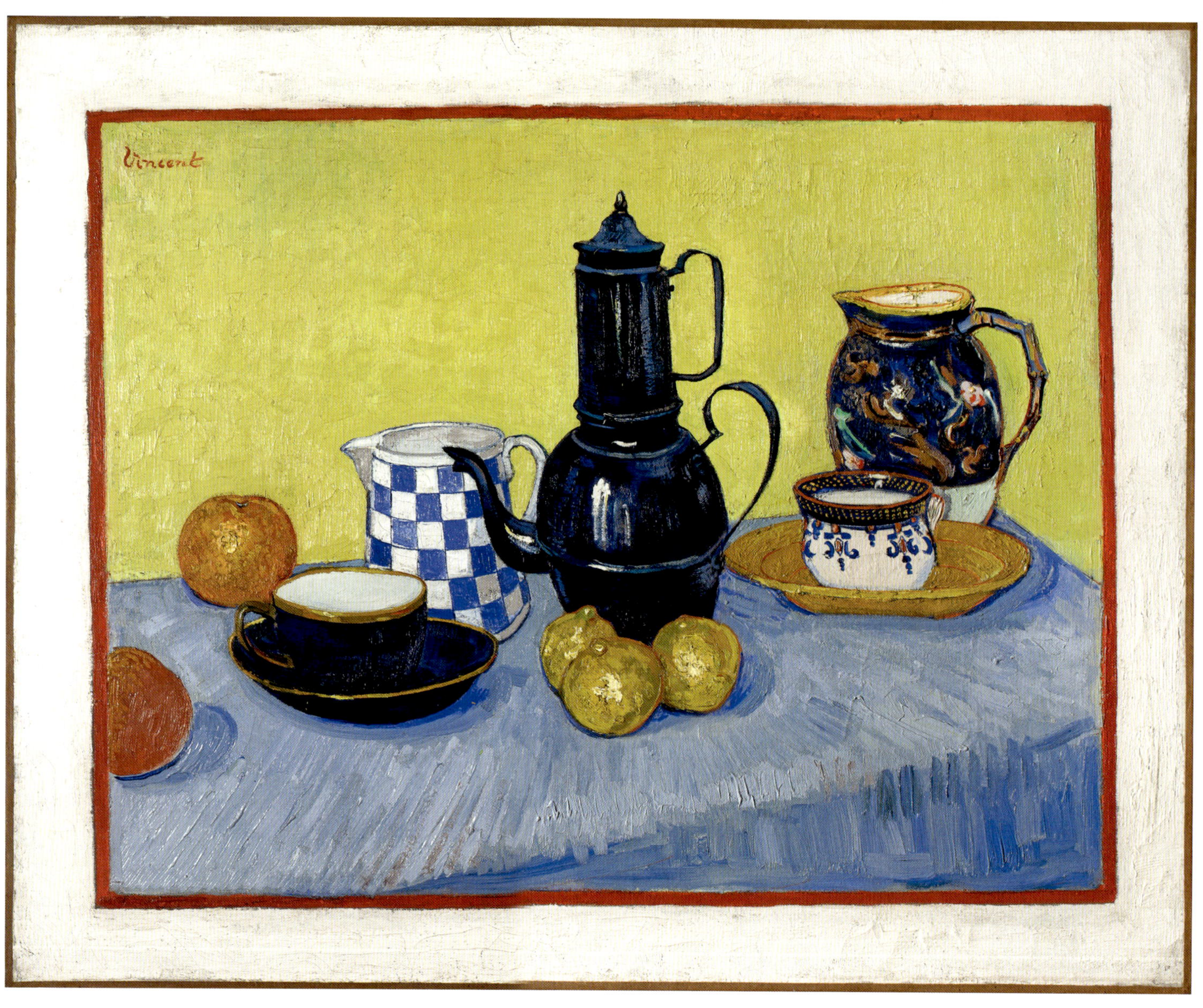

Fig. 28
Vincent van Gogh
Still Life with Coffeepot
Arles, May 1888
Oil on canvas
25⁹⁄₁₆ × 31⁷⁄₈ in. (65 × 81 cm)
Basil & Elise Goulandris Foundation, Athens

Fig. 29
Vincent van Gogh
Still Life
Arles, May 1888
Oil on canvas
21¾ × 18³⁄₁₆ in. (55.2 × 46.2 cm)
The Barnes Foundation, Philadelphia, BF928

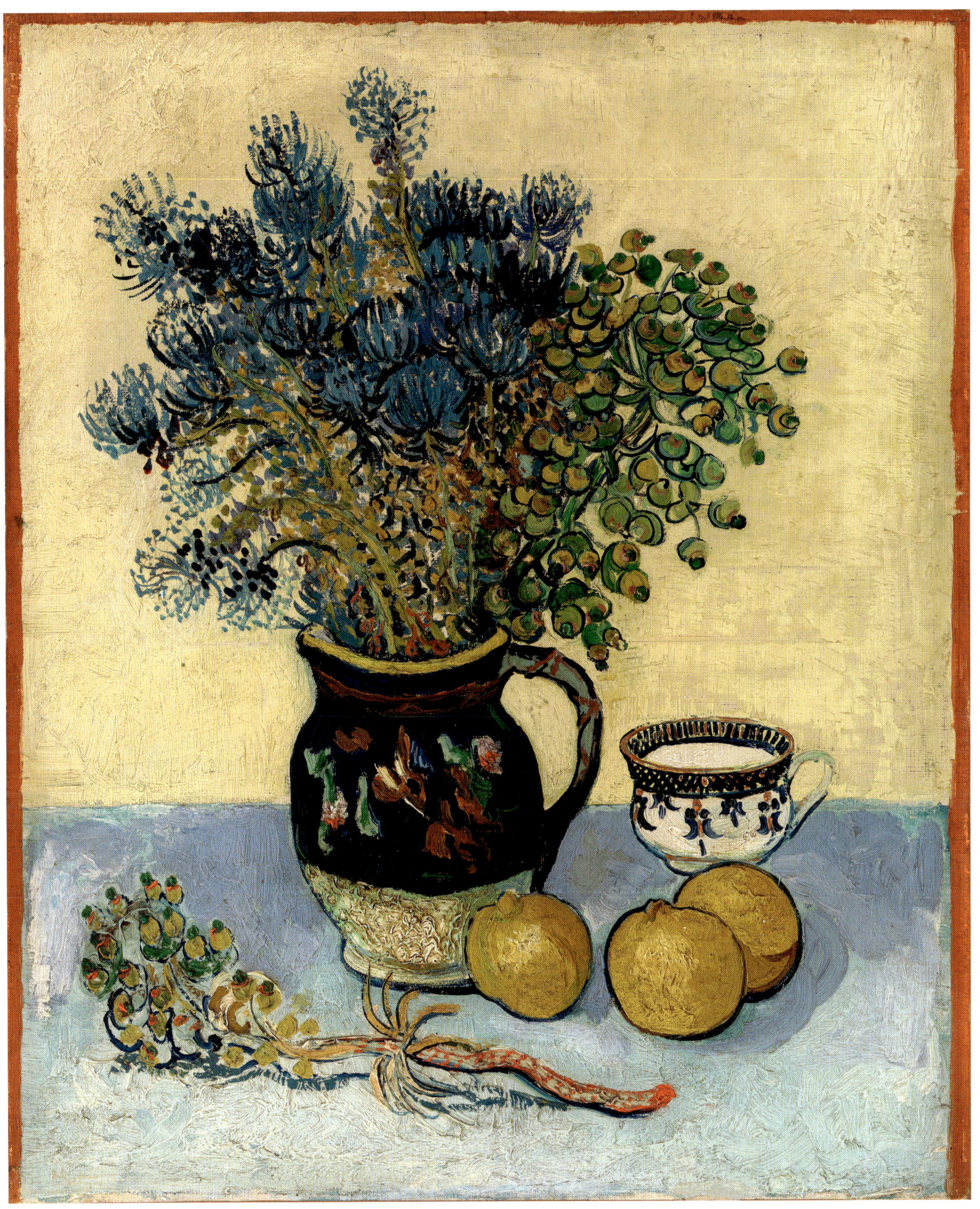

part should be "royal blue," potentially covered in a "blue plush" fabric, similar to a velvet (*fig. 30*).[18] Van Gogh was planning to give the painting to Hermanus Tersteeg, head of the Goupil & Cie gallery at The Hague, and his vision of a royal-blue plush and gold frame may have been intended to marry his bold color theory with a more conservative, upscale interior. The frame was probably never produced, but Van Gogh's sketch nonetheless shows his eager experimentation in Arles with different colors and materials, and his growing interest in coordinating frames to the contexts in which they might be displayed.

By May, Van Gogh had rented the Yellow House, the home that he hoped to transform into the Studio of the South, where fellow artists could visit him and share living costs. The prospect of having a more permanent space in which to display paintings prompted him to consider the relationships between pictures, frames, and their settings more deeply, spurring him to new creative heights. Frames became increasingly essential to his practice, and by October he proclaimed, "I can't finish off except in a frame."[19] As he waited for Paul Gauguin to arrive at the Yellow House (his first and, as it turned out, last guest), he excitedly planned a suite of canvases depicting sunflowers that he described to his friend the artist Émile Bernard as "a decoration" for the house.[20] His choice of the word "decoration" is significant because it suggests his alignment with the then avant-garde ideas that paintings could be decorative rather than narrative or instructive, and that artists could prioritize form and color over subject matter to create immersive and sensorially impactful forms of art.[21] From the project's genesis, he was considering the frames for the sunflower "decoration," writing to Bernard about his plans to create "a decoration in which harsh or broken yellows will burst against various BLUE backgrounds, from the palest Veronese to royal blue, framed with thin laths painted in orange lead."[22] This description of paintings framed with a red-orange pigment calls to mind his earlier experiments with red borders in still lifes such as *Still Life with Coffeepot*, and immediately conjures the way red-orange frames would contrast with the paintings' blues and yellows to dazzle the eye with color.[23]

The type of thin, colorful frame that Van Gogh initially planned for his sunflower paintings is still visible in a

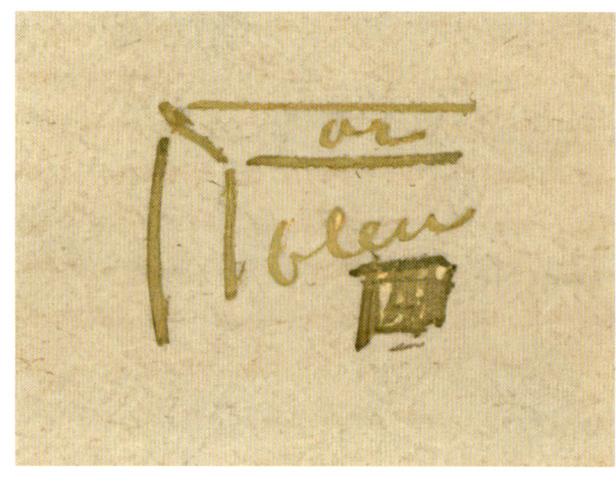

Fig. 30
Vincent van Gogh's sketch of the frame profile for *Bridge at Arles (Pont de Langlois)* (1888; Kröller-Müller Museum, Otterlo, Netherlands), from his letter to Theo van Gogh, Arles, on or about April 3, 1888

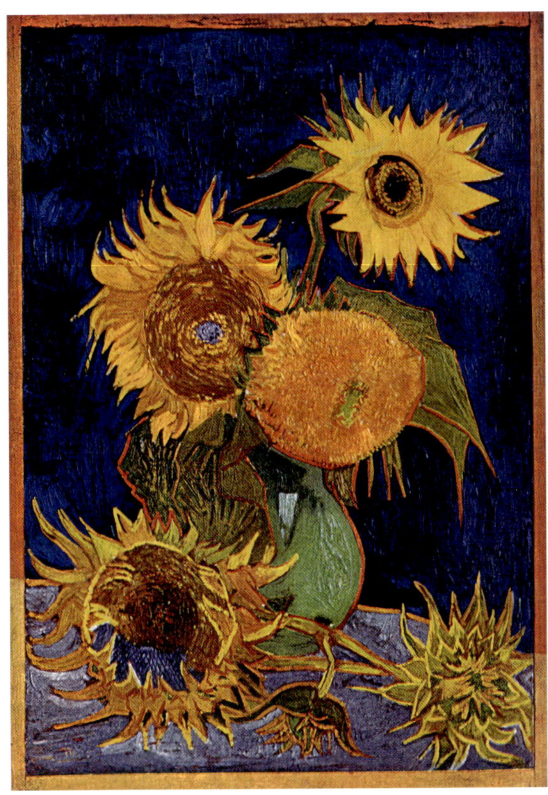

Fig. 31
Vincent van Gogh
Six Sunflowers
Arles, August 1888
Oil on canvas, mounted on panel
$38\frac{9}{16} \times 27\frac{3}{16}$ in. (98 × 69 cm)
Destroyed in World War II; reproduced from a photograph published in 1921 in Tokyo
Archives of Mushakoji Saneatsu Memorial Museum, Tokyo

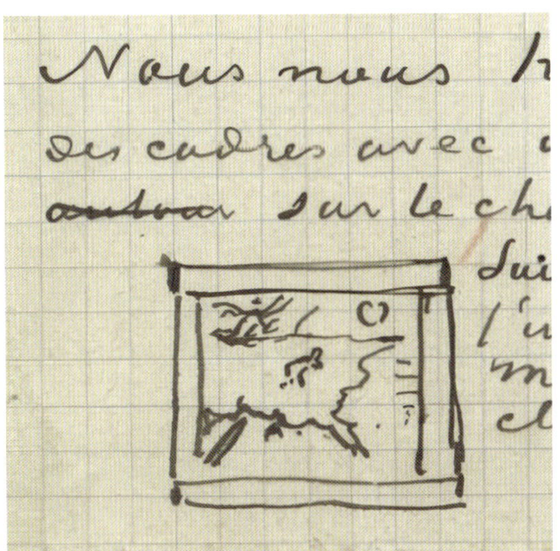
Nous nous
des cadres avec
sur le ch

Fig. 32
Vincent van Gogh's sketch of a frame made from strips of wood, from his letter to Theo van Gogh, Arles, November 10, 1888

surviving photograph of the now-destroyed *Six Sunflowers* (*fig. 31*), one of the four sunflower paintings he completed in August 1888.[24] Van Gogh seems to have nailed four thin pieces of wood directly to the painting's stretcher, leaving the joints clearly visible, which fits with his later description (accompanied by a sketch) of making cheap frames from "simple strips of wood nailed on the stretching frame and *painted*" (*fig. 32*).[25] Riffing on his initial vision of "orange lead" frames, he painted the wood in shades that glow against the rich blue background, shifting from a red orange against the blue wall to a yellow orange against the tabletop. The frame is fully integrated into the composition, echoing and emphasizing the orange and red outlines around the flowers, leaves, and vase, which Van Gogh referred to as a "halo."[26] Framing in the sense of outlining is central to the visual logic of the picture, and the composition would be incomplete without its frame. The frames that no longer survive may have functioned similarly, playfully accenting outlines.

The frames that Van Gogh planned for his sunflower pictures were important not only to his compositions but also to his efforts to shape the Yellow House into an artistic community. Visualizing the red-orange frames in a letter to Bernard, he wrote that he sought to re-create the "effects of *stained-glass windows* of a Gothic church."[27] This reference to stained glass would have surely pleased his friend, who, like Gauguin, drew inspiration from the bright colors and dark outlines of Gothic windows, pioneering a style later called Cloisonnism. The stained-glass metaphor suggests glowing color, but also fits within a larger pattern of Van Gogh using medievalizing language to describe the Studio of the South.[28] For him, the Yellow House was not simply a home with space for visitors but the genesis of a community where "artists would guarantee their livelihood amongst themselves, mutually, and independently of the dealers, each agreeing to give a substantial number of paintings to the society, and . . . earnings as well as losses would be shared."[29] This idea was not entirely impractical, but he also romantically envisioned the house as a space where he and his companions would "join together as the old monks did, . . . living more or less like monks or hermits, with work as our ruling passion."[30] Van Gogh was hardly the first to imagine an artistic community modeled, at least rhetorically, on medieval monasteries. His discussions with Theo about his plans explicitly mention the "English Pre-Raphaelites," artists who emulated medieval art in part because they believed it embodied a model of fulfilling labor at odds with nineteenth-century capitalism.[31] Van Gogh's relationship to medieval art was likewise deeply tied to his social concerns. Following historian Hippolyte Taine, whose works he read avidly, Van Gogh believed that art reflects the society that produces it.[32] He cautioned Bernard against emulating historical styles too literally, advising him to remain in sync with his own era, but he nonetheless believed that medieval art embodied a culture at odds with the "total laxity and anarchy" of the nineteenth century.[33] Likely drawing from the discussions of medieval life in philosopher Thomas Carlyle's *Past and Present* (1843), a book he admired, Van Gogh mused, "I have no doubt that we'll again see an incarnation of this society when the socialists logically build their social edifice."[34] This vision of the medieval (and specifically the monastic) world as a prototype for a socialist utopia was popular among progressives in the period, and is helpful context for understanding Van Gogh's experiments in Arles, including those with frames.

While Van Gogh initially planned to enclose each of the sunflower paintings in a red-orange frame, at least two—likely the London and Munich versions (see pp. 10–11, 14–15)—ended up "surrounded by strips of wood."[35] These frames could have been painted, but his repeated mentions of unpainted wood frames in his letters from Arles suggest that the *Sunflowers* would have been framed similarly. The letters recount Van Gogh's efforts to have local carpenters produce frames made from walnut, chestnut, and pine, and some letters even specify the tones of wood he preferred—for instance, a "yellowed chestnut."[36] He was evidently still attentive to the color harmonies between frame and canvas even when the frame was unpainted. He seems furthermore to have coordinated the wood frames to the furnishings of the Yellow House rooms, using light-colored oak and pine frames in his bedroom to harmonize with his pine furniture, and walnut frames in the guest room to match the walnut furniture.[37] Since the London and Munich *Sunflowers*

Fig. 33
Vincent van Gogh
The Bedroom
Arles, October 1888
Oil on canvas
28½ × 35¹⁵⁄₁₆ in. (72.4 × 91.3 cm)
Van Gogh Museum, Amsterdam
(Vincent van Gogh Foundation)

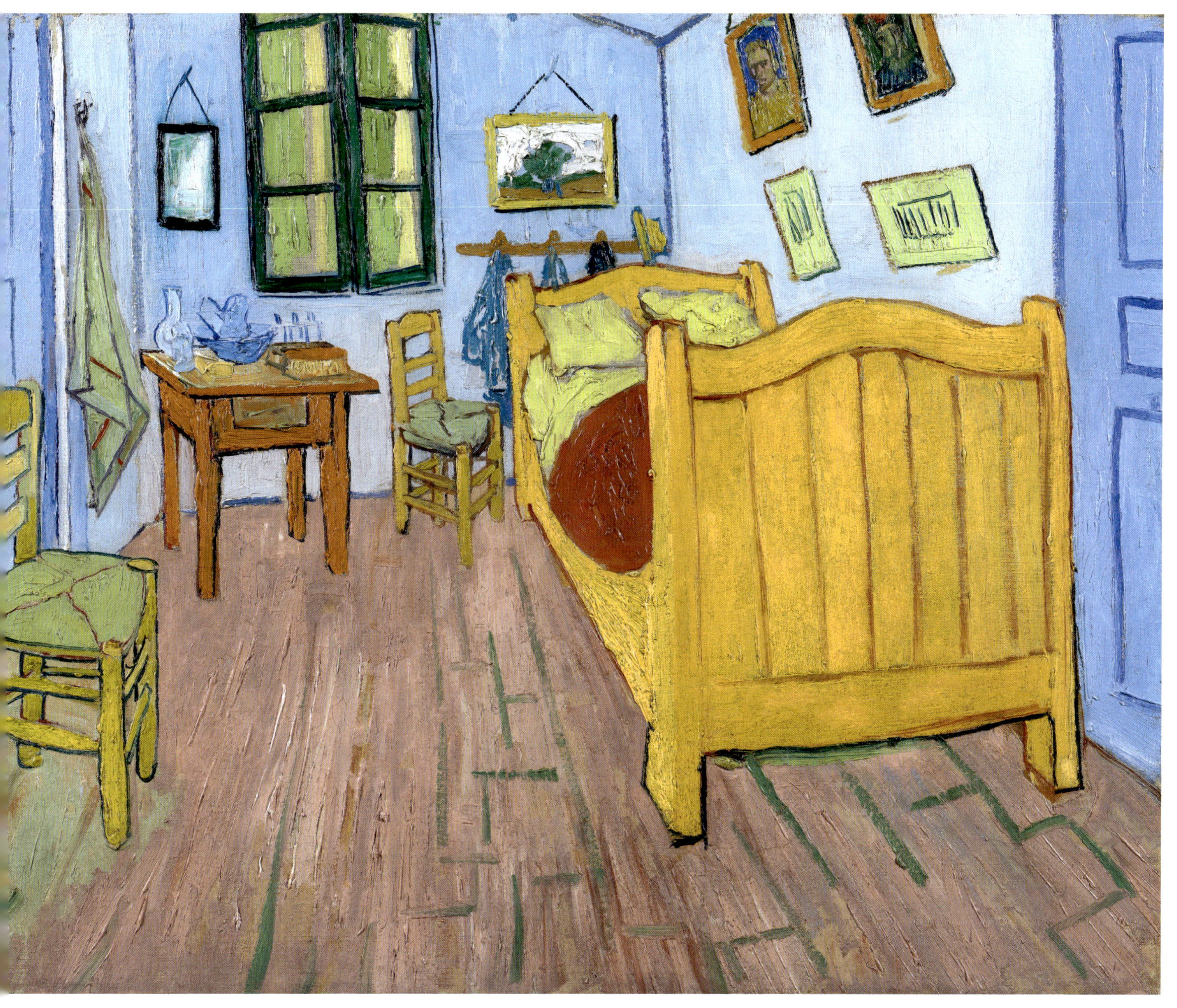

were originally displayed in the guest room, their frames would likely have been walnut, in keeping with the other frames Van Gogh described in the room, such as the one that surrounded *The Poet's Garden* (1888; The Art Institute of Chicago).[38] A rich brown walnut frame would certainly have complemented the pictures compositionally, accentuating the dark rings in the flowers' centers. The correspondences Van Gogh established between his frames and furniture are visible in his painting of his bedroom (*fig. 33*), where shades of yellow articulate both the bed frame and the picture frames above it. The simple wood frames bring the paintings into harmony with the room, making them a part of the Yellow House. Van Gogh boasted of purchasing similarly modest frames for a mere five francs each, but such frames were never simply economic necessities. They were also expressions of his vision for art as a part of humble daily life.[39] In his early letters, he wrote to Theo of his ambition to create works that "ordinary working men" could hang in their "room or workplace."[40] His simply constructed wooden frames asserted that his paintings not only depicted everyday life but also belonged to it. Grounding the paintings in the very environments they portrayed, the Yellow House's frames set Van Gogh apart from Realist or Hague School painters, who surrounded their scenes of rural life in elaborate gilded frames for elite consumption. Van Gogh's humble frames were testaments to his deeply held belief that art should be accessible to everyone.

When Van Gogh first imagined placing paintings of sunflowers in his guest room, he wrote to his sister, "I want to stuff at least 6 very large canvases into this tiny little room, the way the Japanese do, especially the huge bouquets of sunflowers."[41] He had never visited Japan, but his idea of the country, formed from novels, travelogues, and prints, was another important influence on his notions about framing and display in the Yellow House. He associated Arles with the colorful landscapes he saw in Japanese prints, writing in the same letter to his sister, "*I'm in Japan here.*"[42] As Tsukasa Kōdera has discussed, Van Gogh's idea of Japan was essentially utopian.[43] He believed that Japanese artists lived in brotherhood with one another and devoted their days to studying nature, spending hours examining "a single blade of grass."[44] This idea of Japan integrated seamlessly with Van Gogh's vision for the Yellow House, where he even painted a portrait of himself as a bonze, or Buddhist monk.[45] Given Van Gogh's close association of Arles with Japan, it is not surprising that he attempted to emulate Japanese interiors in the Yellow House. When he read Pierre Loti's *Madame Chrysanthème* (1887), a novel set in Japan, he focused on the passages describing Japanese rooms and was particularly struck by accounts of minimally furnished spaces.[46] The most important source for his ideas about the display of artwork in Japan, however, would have been his own collection of

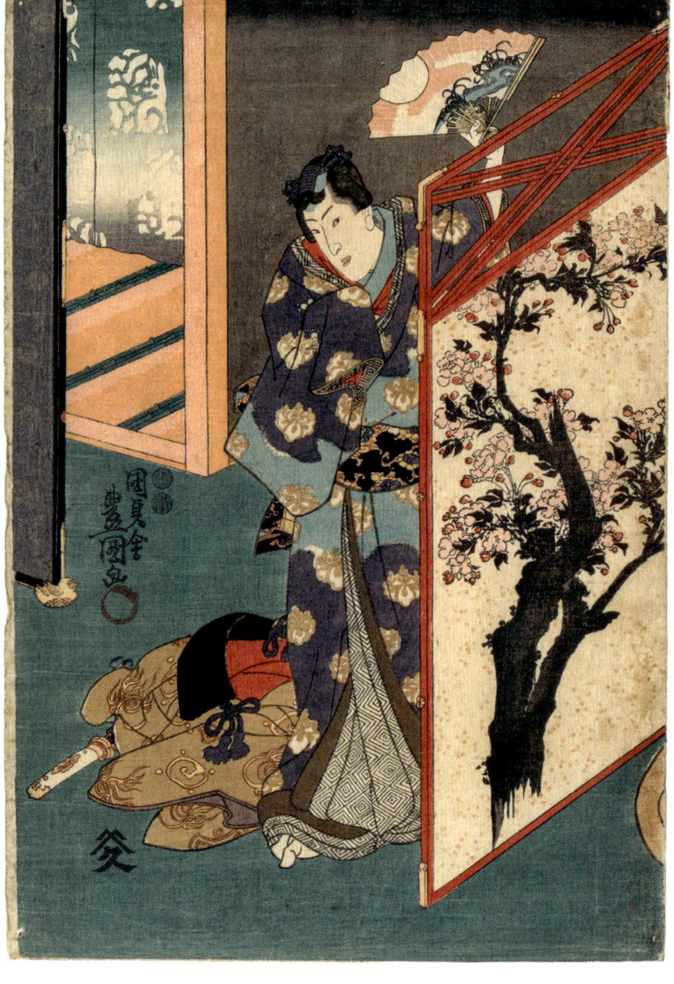

Figs. 34a,b
Utagawa Kunisada I (Japanese, 1786–1865)
Flowers, Birds, Wind, and Moon
1849–52
Color woodcut; left and central sheets of a triptych
Each: 14⁹⁄₁₆ × 10¼ in. (37 × 26 cm)
Van Gogh Museum, Amsterdam
(Vincent van Gogh Foundation)

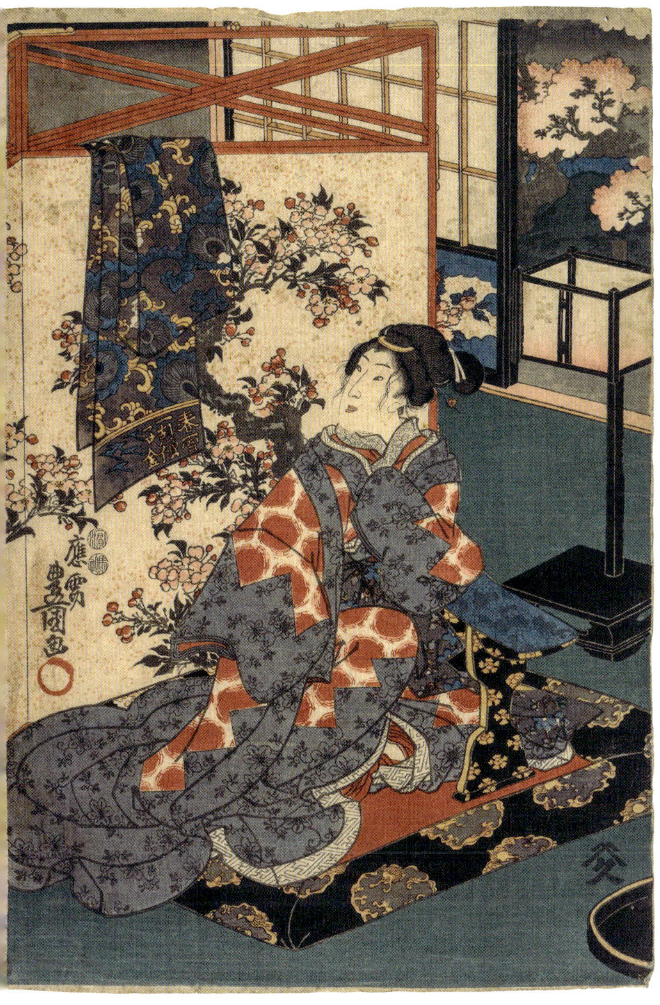

Japanese prints. He possessed, for instance, the left and central sheets of a triptych by Utagawa Kunisada I that depicts a flirtatious encounter between a man and a woman, each positioned on opposite sides of a large folding screen (*figs. 34a,b*).[47] The screen fills the room with painted branches of pink cherry blossoms that echo the flowering trees just visible through the doorway at the far right. All but consumed by floral painting, this interior may have fueled Van Gogh's idea to fill his guest room with paintings of sunflowers, and indeed his early conviction that these pictures should be framed in red orange may have been inspired by the screen's lacquer edge. Later, as his plans for the room's decoration evolved to include four canvases depicting the park outside, he may have been attempting to re-create Japanese interiors punctuated by landscapes glimpsed through sliding doors and windows, as seen in prints in his collection.

Van Gogh's approaches to framing were closely linked to his ideas about Japanese prints. In a letter to Theo about Dutch artists working with heavy architectural frames, he closed by writing, "True, if we're not producing framed paintings like these Dutchmen, you and I, all the same we're making paintings like Japanese prints, and let's keep it to that, no more."[48] The contrast drawn here between "framed paintings" and "paintings like Japanese prints" underscores framing as a means through which Van Gogh sought to distance himself from the European mainstream and ally himself with Japan. His first mention of choosing "a reed frame like a thin strip of wood" for his paintings tellingly comes at the end of a paragraph discussing the interiors described in *Madame Chrysanthème*.[49] Van Gogh clearly associated this type of frame with Japan, and he may have been inspired by the European fashion for displaying Japanese prints in frames made from either red lacquer or thin pieces of bamboo.[50] The painted red borders that appear in his work and that are prevalent in his copies after Japanese prints such as *Flowering Plum Orchard (After Hiroshige)* (1887; Van Gogh Museum, Amsterdam) may even be emulating such frames. In Arles, thin wooden frames, sometimes painted a lacquer-like red, would have created similar visual effects on a larger scale. Another source of inspiration for his frames may have been the colored edges surrounding some of the Japanese prints in his collection, notably those in Utagawa Hiroshige III's album *New Selection of Birds and Flowers* (1871–73; *fig. 35*), where each print has a thin border of blue, green, or yellow. During his time in Arles, Van Gogh was studying this album closely and writing to Theo about his ambition to create a similar folding album.[51] Japanese prints have long been recognized as an important inspiration for Van Gogh's compositions, but the influence of these works on his frames is crucial for understanding how Van Gogh wanted his art to relate to its setting. Frames mediate between paintings and their settings, but in Arles, Van Gogh seized on framing as a medium through which he could attempt to *transform* his setting, making the Yellow House into the Japanesque utopia of his dreams.

Although Van Gogh initially used his sunflower canvases as decorations for his guest room, he began to combine them into new configurations after his mental breakdown and Gauguin's subsequent departure from Arles. In early 1889, he had just completed a portrait of Augustine Roulin, the wife of his postman, who had recently given birth (*fig. 36*). He called the picture *La berceuse*, a French word meaning both "the lullaby" and "the cradle rocker," a reference to the rope he painted her holding, which would have been tied to a cradle. Sketching a diagram at the bottom of a letter, he explained that he wanted to create "a sort of triptych" by placing "the Berceuse in the middle and the two canvases of the sunflowers to the right and the left" (*fig. 37*).[52] He described how the sunflower pictures would act as "standard lamps or candelabra," a comparison that emphasized his sense of the paintings as decorative art.[53] He made note of the pictures' existing frames, explaining that *La berceuse* was in a red frame and the *Sunflowers* in wooden ones.[54] He also assembled a second version of the triptych, intended for Gauguin, which included the version of *La berceuse* (1889) at the Art Institute of Chicago and the Philadelphia and Amsterdam *Sunflowers* (see pp. 22–23, 26–27).[55] Van Gogh did not describe the frames intended for this second triptych, but traces of yellow-orange paint around the edges of the Philadelphia *Sunflowers* suggest that it may have once had a colorful frame, not unlike that which surrounded

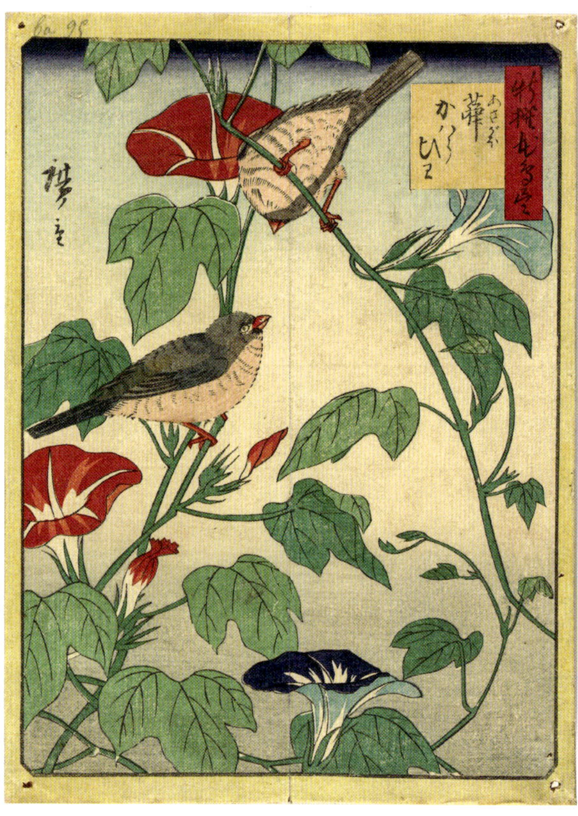

Fig. 35
Utagawa Hiroshige III (Japanese, 1842–1894)
Morning Glory and Oriental Greenfinch
From the album *New Selection of Birds and Flowers*, 1871–73
Color woodcut
9¼ × 6⅞ in. (23.5 × 17.5 cm)
Van Gogh Museum, Amsterdam
(Vincent van Gogh Foundation)

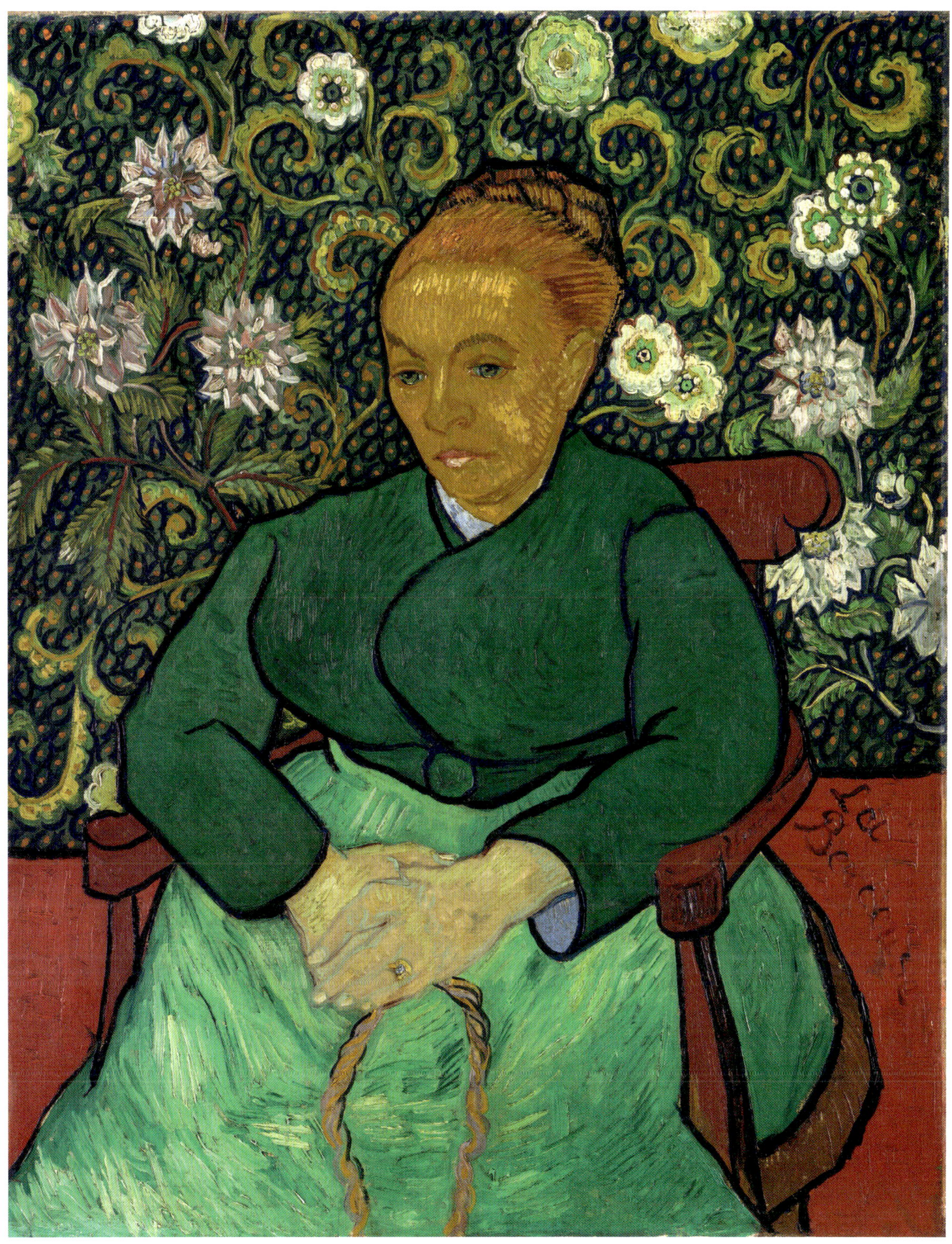

Fig. 36
Vincent van Gogh
La berceuse (Portrait of Madame Roulin)
Arles, December 1888–January 1889
Oil on canvas
$36\frac{1}{4} \times 28\frac{9}{16}$ in. (92 × 72.5 cm)
Kröller-Müller Museum, Otterlo, Netherlands, KM 109.725

Six Sunflowers.[56] In any event, Van Gogh's decorative approach to the triptych form in each of these assemblages transformed his sunflower canvases into an extended frame for *La berceuse*, collapsing the line between painting and frame, and pushing his experiments with framing and display to a new extreme (*fig. 38*).

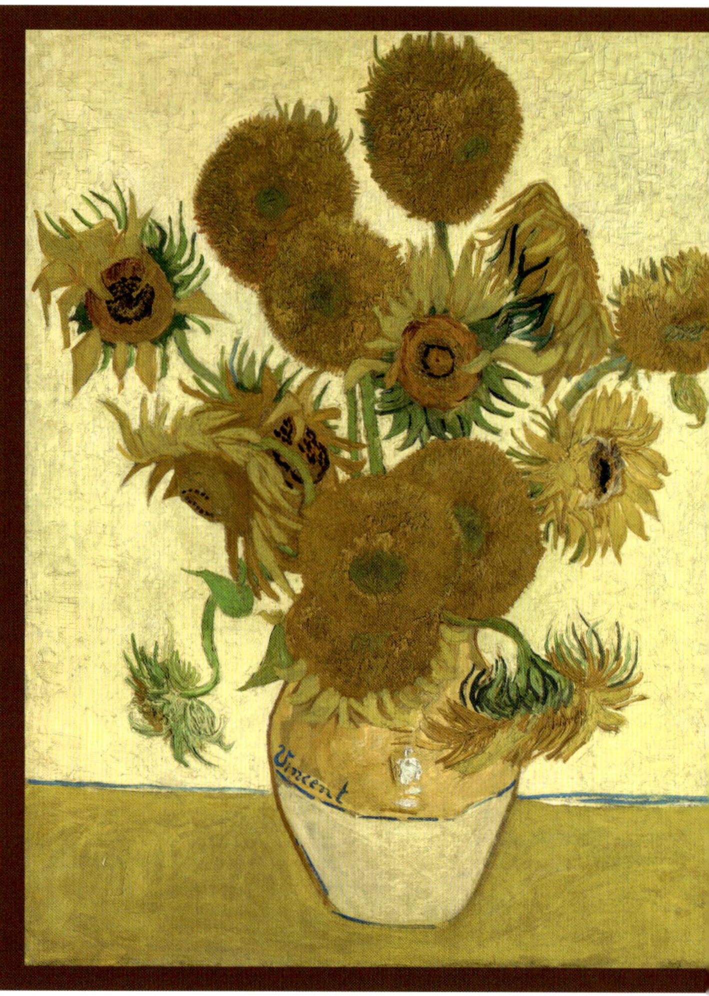

Van Gogh had experimented with triptychs before, arranging his paintings of orchards, for example, into groupings that recalled Japanese print triptychs.[57] The grouping formed by placing *La berceuse* between sunflower paintings, however, evokes a winged altarpiece, transforming Madame Roulin into a modern-day Madonna. The idea for the triptych was specifically inspired by Loti's novel *Pêcheur d'Islande* (1886), a story about Breton fishermen, which Van Gogh had read with Gauguin. He was struck by the way that the sailors in the novel took comfort from a brightly painted ceramic statuette of the Virgin Mary in a "red and blue robe" fastened on a wall with "artificial flowers" nailed beside it.[58] He wrote to Theo, "My idea had been to make a decoration like one for the far end of a cabin on a ship"; it would be "such a picture that sailors, at once children and martyrs, seeing it in the cabin of a boat of Icelandic fishermen, would experience a feeling of being rocked, reminding them of their own lullabies."[59] As Leo Jansen has discussed, one of Van Gogh's primary motivations as an artist was to create works that would "console" the viewer, an ambition not surprising for a minister's son and a former lay preacher.[60] Loti's ceramic Virgin offered Van Gogh a model for a ubiquitous, everyday art capable of eliciting a profound emotional response from its viewers. Framing *La berceuse* with *Sunflowers*, he transformed the portrait from a simple portrayal of a neighbor to something more universal that viewers could experience in a personal, spiritual way.

The vivid surface of the ceramic Virgin in Loti's text resonates with Van Gogh's approach to color in the triptych. Building upon his earlier experiments with bright, contrasting frames, Van Gogh was interested in the decorative play of color across the triptych, explaining how "the yellow and orange tones of the head take on more brilliance through the proximity of the yellow shutters."[61] These vivid color contrasts, no doubt heightened by the

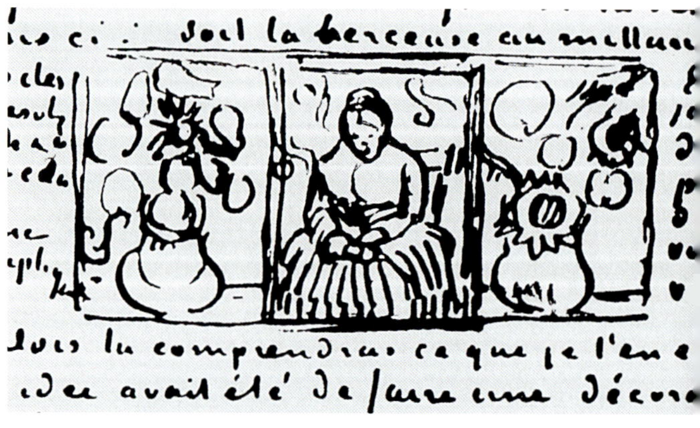

Fig. 37
Vincent van Gogh's sketch of a triptych comprising a portrait of Augustine Roulin as *La berceuse* flanked by sunflower paintings, from his letter to Theo van Gogh, Saint-Rémy-de-Provence, on or about May 23, 1889

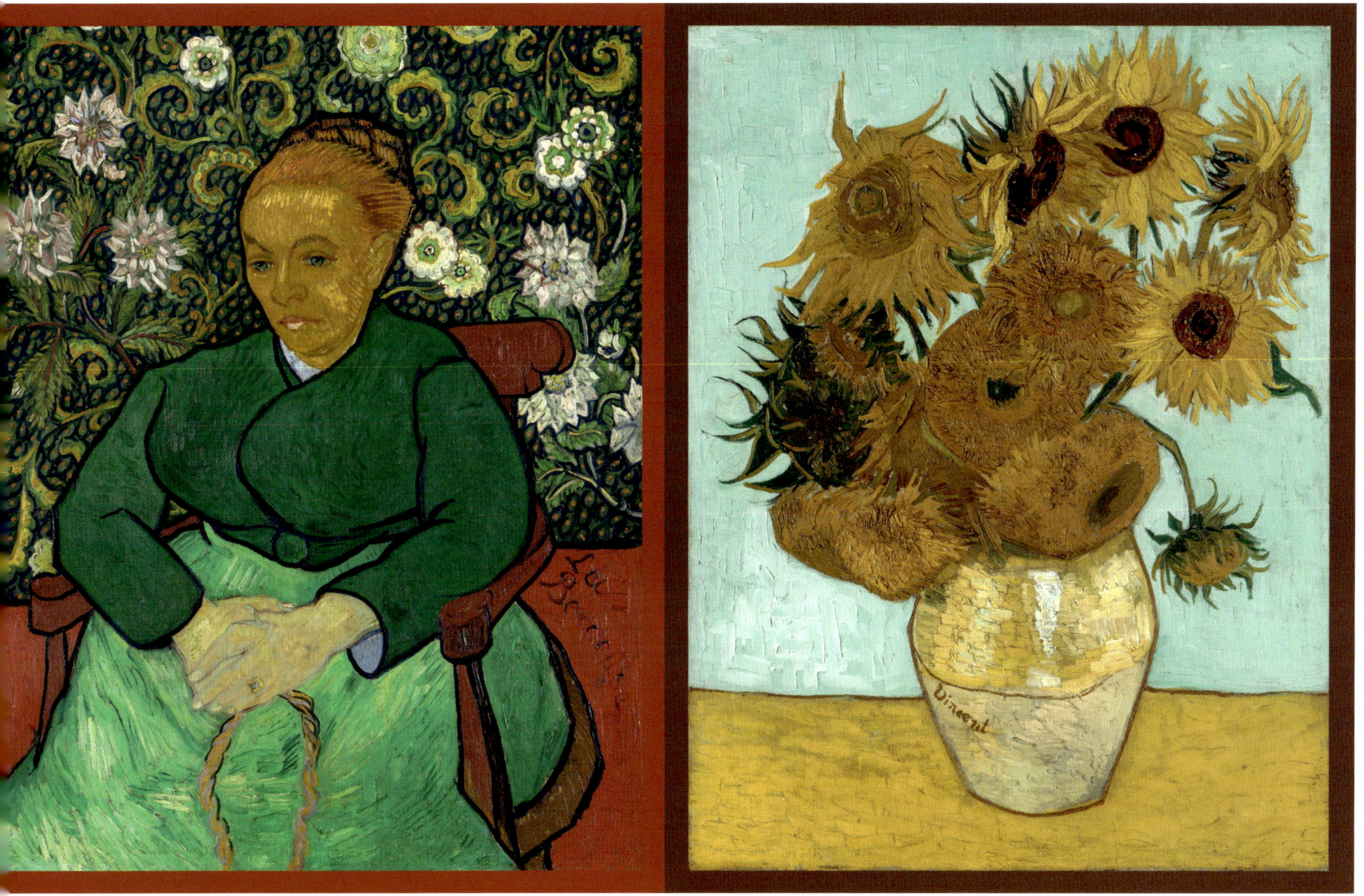

Fig. 38
Triptych with Vincent van Gogh's *La berceuse (Portrait of Madame Roulin)* (see *fig. 36*) flanked by (left and right) the London and Munich *Sunflowers* (see pp. 10–11, 14–15), with colored borders digitally added to simulate frames

red frame surrounding *La berceuse*, were central to the way he envisioned his work as updating historical traditions of religious art. He wrote, "I'd like to paint men or women with that *je ne sais quoi* of the eternal, of which the halo used to be the symbol, and which we try to achieve through the radiance itself, through the vibrancy of our colorations."[62] He later elaborated, "Had I had the strength to continue, I'd have done portraits of saints and of holy women from life, and who would have appeared to be from another century and they would be citizens of the present day, and yet would have had something in common with very primitive Christians."[63] The association of vibrant color with spiritual art recalls Van Gogh's early descriptions of his plans to frame the sunflower pictures in red to simulate the "effects of *stained-glass windows* of a Gothic church."[64] His return to this idea at the end of his time at the Yellow House is a poignant reaffirmation of his ideals even as his dream for creating a utopian community was coming apart.

The triptych ultimately embodies what Debora Silverman has called Van Gogh's "sacred realism," his efforts to create spiritually meaningful imagery rooted in ordinary, secular life.[65] Casting a postman's wife as a saint or Madonna, the triptych becomes a powerful humanist assertion of the dignity of everyday people. Framed by humble vases of sunflowers gathered from her neighborhood, Madame Roulin is embedded in nineteenth-century Arles even as the glowing colors and triptych form allude to the eternal. In an altarpiece, a frame typically marks a boundary between the worshipper and the divine image, but Van Gogh's *Sunflowers* root *La berceuse* in the viewer's ordinary, secular space. Conceived at a moment when the Yellow House experiment was coming to a close, the gesture of transforming the sunflower canvases into frames distilled his ideals. No longer was he interested in imagining himself as a Gothic or Japanese monk; instead, at a moment of personal instability and crisis, his ambition came down to a simple desire to provide solace through his paintings, surrounding them with frames that acted not as boundaries to the viewer but as invitations.

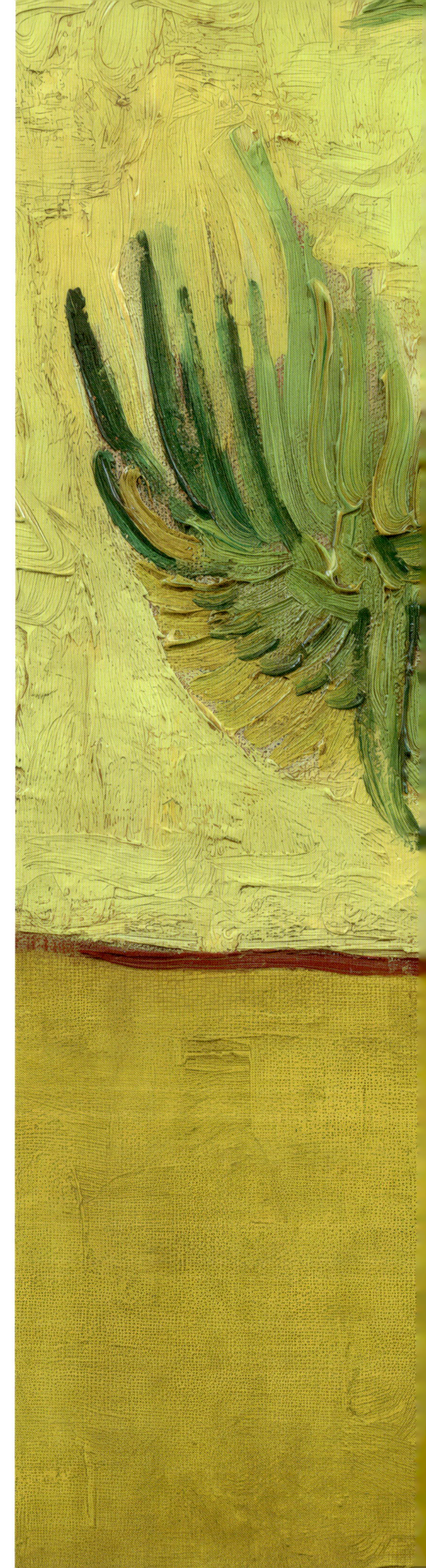

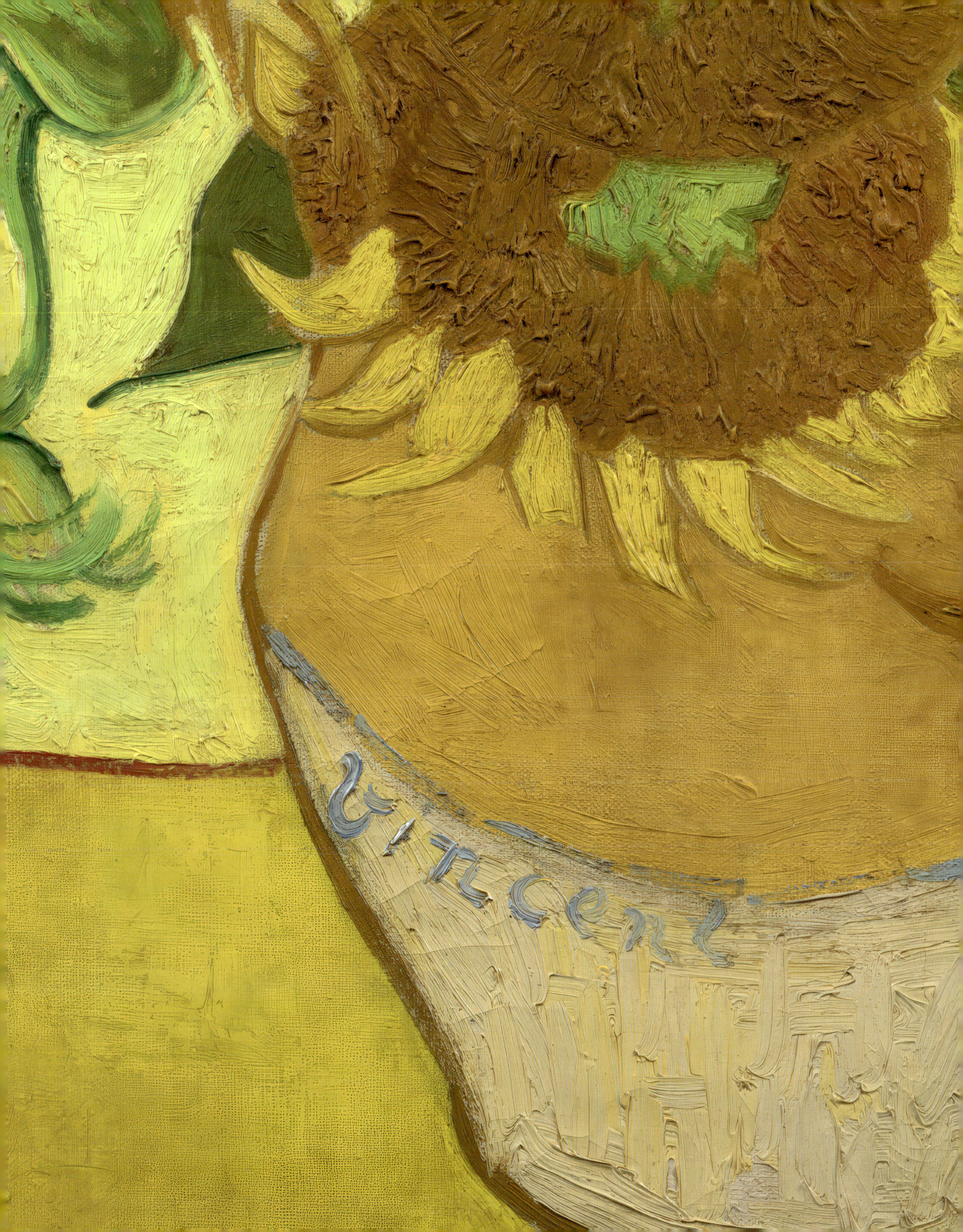
Vincent

1. By my count, there are conservatively fifty-six surviving letters from Van Gogh that discuss frames, twenty-six of which date from his time in Arles. For his letters, see *Vincent van Gogh: The Letters*, ed. Leo Jansen, Hans Luijten, and Nienke Bakker (Van Gogh Museum & Huygens ING, 2009), online version December 2024, https://vangoghletters.org. All correspondence to or from Van Gogh cited herein is from this source. This essay's opening quotation is from Vincent van Gogh to Theo van Gogh, Nuenen, Netherlands, on or about March 2, 1884, letter 432 (emphasis in original).
2. For an overview of evolving frame styles in the second half of the nineteenth century, see Eva A. Mendgen, ed., *In Perfect Harmony: Picture + Frame, 1850–1920*, exh. cat. (Van Gogh Museum, 1995).
3. Van Gogh likely saw Seurat's *A Sunday on La Grande Jatte* (1884; The Art Institute of Chicago) in the 1886 Impressionist exhibition, held at the Maison Dorée in Paris. He probably saw the picture again, along with Seurat's *Models* (1886–88; The Barnes Foundation, Philadelphia), when he visited Seurat's studio with his brother Theo on February 19, 1888, just hours before he departed for Arles. He later praised the inventiveness of Seurat's frames. See Vincent van Gogh to Paul Gauguin, Arles, October 3, 1888, letter 695; and Vincent van Gogh to Theo van Gogh, Arles, October 17, 1888, letter 707.
4. For more on the philosophy of "art for art's sake," see Elizabeth Prettejohn, *Art for Art's Sake: Aestheticism in Victorian Painting* (Yale University Press, 2008).
5. See Martha Ward, "Impressionist Installations and Private Exhibitions," *Art Bulletin* 73, no. 4 (December 1991): 599–622, https://doi.org/10.2307/3045832; and David Park Curry, "Total Control: Whistler at an Exhibition," in *James McNeill Whistler: A Reexamination*, ed. Ruth E. Fine, Studies in the History of Art 19 (National Gallery of Art, 1987), 67–82.
6. Goupil & Cie maintained a framing workshop; see Pierre-Lin Renié, "The Image on the Wall: Prints as Decoration in Nineteenth-Century Interiors," *Nineteenth-Century Art Worldwide* 5, no. 2 (Autumn 2006), https://www.19thc-artworldwide.org/autumn06/the-image-on-the-wall-prints-as-decoration-in-nineteenth-century-interiors.
7. Vincent van Gogh to Theo van Gogh, Nuenen, Netherlands, on or about March 2, 1884, letter 432.
8. Vincent van Gogh to Theo van Gogh, letter 432.
9. "As regards the potato eaters—it's a painting *that looks well in gold*, I'm sure of that"; Vincent van Gogh to Theo van Gogh, Nuenen, Netherlands, April 30, 1885, letter 497 (emphasis in original).
10. Charles Blanc, *Grammaire des arts du dessin: Architecture, sculpture, peinture* (Jules Renouard, 1867), 597–602; and Mariella Guzzoni, *Vincent's Books: Van Gogh and the Writers Who Inspired Him* (University of Chicago Press, 2020), 78–81.
11. Van Gogh would certainly have been aware of such frames by 1887: Not only were Seurat's experimental frames highlights of the 1886 Impressionist exhibition, but Degas had occasionally used red and green frames throughout the 1880s (for instance, the green frame that still surrounds *Bather Lying on the Ground* [c. 1885; Musée d'Orsay, Paris]), and Camille Pissarro, whom Van Gogh particularly admired, had painted frames with a variety of colors in the early 1880s. For an overview of these trends, see Isabelle Cahn, *Cadres de peintres* (Hermann, 1989).
12. For a chronology of Van Gogh's experiments with painted borders, see Marieke Jooren, "Van Gogh's Finishing Touches: Varnish, Signatures, Frames and Painted Borders," in *Van Gogh's Studio Practice*, ed. Marije Vellekoop et al. (Van Gogh Museum, 2013), 302–5.
13. The frame's red edge was still present when Van Gogh included the still life in the second of three portraits of Parisian color merchant Julien Tanguy, completed in 1887 (private collection). Louis van Tilborgh, "Framing van Gogh, 1880–1990," in Mendgen, *In Perfect Harmony*, 164; see also Jooren, "Van Gogh's Finishing Touches," 301.
14. Van Tilborgh, "Framing Van Gogh," 164.
15. Two known examples are Van Gogh's portrait of Alexander Reid in the Kelvingrove Art Gallery and Museum in Glasgow, which has traces of yellow paint along the edges, and *Park at Asnières in Spring* (1887; private collection), which has traces of orange-red paint; Van Tilborgh, 164.
16. Vincent van Gogh to Theo van Gogh, Arles, May 10, 1888, letter 608.
17. Cindy Kang, "Van Gogh's *Décoration*: Sources of Inspiration," in *Van Gogh: Poets & Lovers*, ed. Cornelia Homburg and Christopher Riopelle, exh. cat. (National Gallery Global, 2024), 134.
18. Vincent van Gogh to Theo van Gogh, Arles, on or about April 3, 1888, letter 592.
19. Vincent van Gogh to Theo van Gogh, Arles, October 8, 1888, letter 699.
20. Vincent van Gogh to Émile Bernard, Arles, August 21, 1888, letter 665.
21. For more on the significance of this project, see Roland Dorn, *Décoration: Vincent van Goghs Werkreihe für das Gelbe Haus in Arles* (Georg Olms Verlag, 1990). For a discussion of the sources that inspired Van Gogh's notion of decoration, see Kang, "Van Gogh's *Décoration*."
22. Van Gogh to Bernard, Arles, August 21, 1888, letter 665 (emphasis in original).
23. Van Gogh typically referred to red lead as "orange lead" and is likely describing a frame that would have been closer to red than orange. For more on Van Gogh's palette and the way he described pigments, see Ella Hendriks, "Sunflowers Up Close," in Nienke Bakker and Ella Hendriks, *Van Gogh and the Sunflowers: A Masterpiece Examined*, exh. cat. (Van Gogh Museum, 2019), 63.
24. This significant discovery was made by Martin Bailey; see Martin Bailey, *The Sunflowers Are Mine: The Story of Van Gogh's Masterpiece* (Frances Lincoln, 2013).
25. Vincent van Gogh to Theo van Gogh, Arles, November 10, 1888, letter 718 (emphasis in original).
26. Vincent van Gogh to Theo van Gogh, Arles, August 23 or 24, 1888, letter 668.
27. Van Gogh to Bernard, Arles, August 21, 1888, letter 665 (emphasis in original).
28. Van Gogh's interest in medievalism is noted by Tsukasa Kōdera, who draws out parallels with the German Nazarene movement; Tsukasa Kōdera, "Japan as Primitivistic Utopia: Van Gogh's Japonisme Portraits," *Simiolus: Netherlands Quarterly for the History of Art* 14, nos. 3–4 (1984): 189, https://doi.org/10.2307/3780577.
29. Vincent van Gogh to Theo van Gogh, Arles, on or about June 15 and 16, 1888, letter 625.
30. Vincent van Gogh to Theo van Gogh, on or about August 13, 1888, letter 660.
31. Vincent van Gogh to Theo van Gogh, Arles, on or about June 15 and 16, 1888, letter 625. For a recent overview of the social dimensions of Pre-Raphaelite practice, see Martin Ellis, Victoria Osborne, and Tim Barringer, *Victorian Radicals: From the Pre-Raphaelites to the Arts & Crafts Movement*, exh. cat. (American Federation of Arts, 2018).
32. Hippolyte Taine, *Philosophie de l'art: Leçons professées à l'École des Beaux-Arts* (Germer Baillière, 1865).
33. Van Gogh to Bernard, Arles, August 5, 1888, letter 655.
34. Van Gogh to Bernard, letter 655. In a letter of 1882, Van Gogh directly quoted Carlyle's *Past and Present*: "Blessed is he who has found his work"; Vincent van Gogh to Theo van Gogh, The Hague, November 26 and 27, 1882, letter 288. For the original, see Thomas Carlyle, *Past and Present* (Chapman and Hall, 1843), 169, https://archive.org/details/pastpresent01carl.
35. Vincent van Gogh to Theo van Gogh, Saint-Rémy-de-Provence, on or about May 23, 1889, letter 776. When Theo later added white frames to these pictures, he kept the inner strips of wood visible, likely to preserve the original color harmonies; Theo van Gogh to Vincent van Gogh, Paris, December 8, 1889, letter 825.

36. Vincent van Gogh to Theo van Gogh, Arles, October 8, 1888, letter 699.
37. The observation that Van Gogh coordinated his wood frames to the Yellow House furnishings appears in Van Tilborgh, "Framing Van Gogh," 168. For the furniture in the respective bedrooms, see Vincent van Gogh to Theo van Gogh, Arles, September 9, 1888, letter 677. For the frames intended for these spaces, see, for example, Vincent van Gogh to Theo van Gogh, Arles, September 18, 1888, letter 683.
38. Vincent van Gogh to Theo van Gogh, Arles, October 8, 1888, letter 699.
39. Vincent van Gogh to Theo van Gogh, Arles, October 17, 1888, letter 707.
40. Vincent van Gogh to Theo van Gogh, The Hague, November 16 or 17, 1882, letter 283.
41. Vincent van Gogh to Willemien van Gogh, Arles, September 14, 1888, letter 678.
42. Vincent van Gogh to Willemien van Gogh, letter 678 (emphasis in original).
43. For Van Gogh's utopian vision of Japan, see Kōdera, "Japan as Primitivistic Utopia." For accounts of Van Gogh's collection of Japanese prints and its importance in his artistic practice, see Chris Uhlenbeck, Louis van Tilborgh, and Shigeru Oikawa, *Japanese Prints: The Collection of Vincent van Gogh* (Thames & Hudson, 2018); and Louis van Tilborgh et al., *Van Gogh & Japan*, exh. cat. (Van Gogh Museum, 2018). For more on Van Gogh's reading about Japan during his time in Arles, see Guzzoni, *Vincent's Books*, 121–44.
44. Vincent van Gogh to Theo van Gogh, Arles, September 24, 1888, letter 686.
45. This self-portrait is in the collection of the Harvard Art Museums, Cambridge, Massachusetts (acc. no. 1951.65). For Van Gogh's description of the painting as a bonze, see Van Gogh to Gauguin, Arles, October 3, 1888, letter 695.
46. Vincent van Gogh to Theo van Gogh, Arles, on or about July 13, 1888, letter 639; and Pierre Loti, *Madame Chrysanthème* (1887; Calmann-Lévy, 1888), 29–30, https://archive.org/details/bnf-bpt6k62124889.
47. The scene is from Ryutei Tanehiko's serial novel *An Imposter Murasaki and a Rustic Genji* (1829–42), a parody of Murasaki Shikibu's eleventh-century novel, *The Tale of Genji*. Where the original novel traced Prince Genji's romances with women of the court, the updated story recounted an elegant gentleman's adventures in the pleasure quarters of Edo (present-day Tokyo).
48. Vincent van Gogh to Theo van Gogh, Arles, October 17, 1888, letter 707.
49. Vincent van Gogh to Theo van Gogh, Arles, on or about July 13, 1888, letter 639.
50. Louis van Tilborgh, "In the Light of Japan: Van Gogh's Quest for Happiness and a Modern Identity," in *Van Gogh & Japan*, ed. Louis van Tilborgh et al., exh. cat. (Van Gogh Museum, 2018), 69.
51. Vincent van Gogh to Theo van Gogh, Arles, May 28, 1888, letter 615.
52. Vincent van Gogh to Theo van Gogh, Saint-Rémy-de-Provence, on or about May 23, 1889, letter 776. In an earlier letter, Van Gogh described arrangements of versions of the *Sunflowers* and *La berceuse* totaling "7 or 9 canvases." His phrasing is ambiguous. He may have been describing a group of canvases that included two or three triptychs (he was planning a third *La berceuse* and was likely toying with whether to paint sunflowers to accompany it). Alternatively, he may have imagined a line of seven or nine alternating pictures, or even, as Roland Dorn has suggested, a radial arrangement of sunflower pictures surrounding a single *La berceuse*. Given that Van Gogh only ever sketched a triptych arrangement, however, the first possibility seems most likely. See Vincent van Gogh to Theo van Gogh, Arles, January 28, 1889, letter 743, n6; see also Dorn, *Décoration*, 306n469.
53. Vincent van Gogh to Theo van Gogh, Arles, January 28, 1889, letter 743.
54. Vincent van Gogh to Theo van Gogh, Saint-Rémy-de-Provence, on or about May 23, 1889, letter 776.
55. Gauguin seems never to have received the sunflower canvases; see Louis van Tilborgh and Ella Hendriks, "The Tokyo *Sunflowers*: A Genuine Repetition by Van Gogh or a Schuffenecker Forgery?," *Van Gogh Museum Journal*, 2001, pp. 24–26, accessed October 18, 2025, https://www.dbnl.org/tekst/_van012200101_01/_van012200101_01_0003.php.
56. These minute traces of yellow-orange paint along the Philadelphia picture's edges became visible when conservator Teresa Lignelli removed tape from the canvas's edges in July 2025. They may be evidence of a colorful original frame or could be residue from touch-ups to later frames. The canvas's tacking margins were removed when the picture was taken off its original stretcher and relined in the mid-twentieth century.
57. For Van Gogh's sketch of three orchard paintings arranged in a triptych-like formation, see Vincent van Gogh to Theo van Gogh, Arles, on or about April 13, 1888, letter 597. The three paintings likely are *The Pink Orchard* (1888), *The Pink Peach Tree* (1888), and *The White Orchard* (1888), all in the collection of the Van Gogh Museum, Amsterdam. Van Gogh owned several Japanese print triptychs depicting cherry blossom scenery, including Utagawa Yoshitora's *Three Women with Sails and Cherry Blossoms* (1846–48), also in the Van Gogh Museum.
58. Pierre Loti, *An Iceland Fisherman* (*Pêcheur d'Islande*), trans. Clara Cadiot (John and Robert Maxwell, 1888), 4.
59. Vincent van Gogh to Theo van Gogh, Saint-Rémy-de-Provence, on or about May 23, 1889, letter 776; and Arles, January 28, 1889, letter 743.
60. Leo Jansen, "Vincent van Gogh's Belief in Art as Consolation," in *Van Gogh's Imaginary Museum: Exploring the Artist's Inner World*, ed. Chris Stolwijk et al., exh. cat. (Van Gogh Museum, 2003).
61. Vincent van Gogh to Theo van Gogh, Saint-Rémy-de-Provence, on or about May 23, 1889, letter 776. On Van Gogh's idea of the sunflower paintings as shutters, see Thompson's essay in this volume, p. 49n40.
62. Vincent van Gogh to Theo van Gogh, Arles, September 3, 1888, letter 673.
63. Vincent van Gogh to Theo van Gogh, Saint-Rémy-de-Provence, September 10, 1889, letter 801.
64. Van Gogh to Bernard, Arles, August 21, 1888, letter 665 (emphasis in original).
65. Debora Silverman, "Framing Art and Sacred Realism: Van Gogh's Ways of Seeing Arles," *Van Gogh Museum Journal*, 2001, pp. 44–61, accessed October 18, 2025, https://www.dbnl.org/tekst/_van012200101_01/_van012200101_01_0004.php; and Debora Silverman, *Van Gogh and Gauguin: The Search for Sacred Art* (Farrar, Straus and Giroux, 2000).

"You talk to me in your letter about a canva
background—to say that it would give yo
that you've made a bad choice."

—Vincent van Gogh to Paul Gauguin
January 21, 1889

f mine, the sunflowers with a yellow
ome pleasure to receive it. I don't think

Further Reading

Bailey, Martin. *Studio of the South: Van Gogh in Provence.* Frances Lincoln, 2016.

Bailey, Martin. *The Sunflowers Are Mine: The Story of Van Gogh's Masterpiece.* Frances Lincoln, 2013.

Bakker, Nienke, Emmanuel Coquery, Teio Meedendorp, and Louis van Tilborgh. *Van Gogh in Auvers-sur-Oise: His Final Months.* Exh. cat., Van Gogh Museum, Amsterdam. Thames & Hudson, 2023.

Bakker, Nienke, and Katie Hanson, eds. *Van Gogh: The Roulin Family Portraits.* Exh. cat. MFA Publications, 2025.

Bakker, Nienke, and Ella Hendriks. *Van Gogh and the Sunflowers: A Masterpiece Examined.* Exh. cat. Van Gogh Museum, 2019.

Cahn, Isabelle. *Cadres de peintres.* Hermann, 1989.

Coyle, Laura. "The Still-Life Paintings of Vincent van Gogh and Their Context." PhD diss., Princeton University, 2007.

Dorn, Roland. *Décoration: Vincent van Goghs Werkreihe für das Gelbe Haus in Arles.* Georg Olms Verlag, 1990.

Druick, Douglas W., and Peter Kort Zegers. *Van Gogh and Gauguin: The Studio of the South.* Exh. cat. Art Institute of Chicago, 2001.

Gayford, Martin. *Van Gogh: Sunflowers.* National Gallery Global, 2024.

Groom, Gloria, ed. *Van Gogh's Bedrooms.* Exh. cat. Art Institute of Chicago, 2016.

Guzzoni, Mariella. *Vincent's Books: Van Gogh and the Writers Who Inspired Him.* University of Chicago Press, 2020.

Hendriks, Ella, and Marije Vellekoop, eds. *Van Gogh's Sunflowers Illuminated: Art Meets Science.* Amsterdam University Press, 2019.

Hoenigswald, Ann. "Vincent van Gogh: His Frames, and the Presentation of Paintings." *Burlington Magazine* 130, no. 1022 (May 1988): 367–72.

Homburg, Cornelia, and Christopher Riopelle, eds. *Van Gogh: Poets & Lovers.* Exh. cat. National Gallery Global, 2024.

Hulsker, Jan. *The New Complete Van Gogh: Paintings, Drawings, Sketches; Revised and Enlarged Edition of the Catalogue Raisonné of the Works of Vincent van Gogh.* J. M. Meulenhoff, 1996.

Jansen, Leo, Hans Luijten, and Nienke Bakker, eds. *Vincent van Gogh: The Letters.* Van Gogh Museum & Huygens ING, online version December 2024. https://vangoghletters.org.

Kōdera, Tsukasa. "Japan as Primitivistic Utopia: Van Gogh's Japonisme Portraits." *Simiolus: Netherlands Quarterly for the History of Art* 14, nos. 3–4 (1984): 189–208. https://doi.org/10.2307/3780577.

Mendgen, Eva A., ed. *In Perfect Harmony: Picture + Frame, 1850–1920*. Exh. cat. Van Gogh Museum, 1995.

Mitchell, Paul, and Lynn Roberts. *A History of European Picture Frames*. Paul Mitchell, 1996.

Pickvance, Ronald. *Van Gogh in Arles*. Exh. cat. Metropolitan Museum of Art, 1984.

Rathbone, Eliza E., William H. Robinson, Elizabeth Steele, and Marcia Steele. *Van Gogh Repetitions*. Exh. cat., Phillips Collection, Washington, DC. Yale University Press, 2013.

Rathbone, Eliza E., and George T. M. Shackelford. *Impressionist Still Life*. H. N. Abrams, 2001.

Silverman, Debora. "Framing Art and Sacred Realism: Van Gogh's Ways of Seeing Arles." *Van Gogh Museum Journal*, 2001, pp. 44–61. https://www.dbnl.org/tekst/_van012200101_01/_van012200101_01_0004.php.

Silverman, Debora. *Van Gogh and Gauguin: The Search for Sacred Art*. Farrar, Straus and Giroux, 2000.

Stolwijk, Chris, Sjraar van Heugten, Leo Jansen, and Andreas Blühm, eds. *Van Gogh's Imaginary Museum: Exploring the Artist's Inner World*. Exh. cat. Van Gogh Museum, 2003.

Tilborgh, Louis van, Nienke Bakker, Cornelia Homburg, Tsukasa Kōdera, and Chris Uhlenbeck. *Van Gogh & Japan*. Exh. cat. Van Gogh Museum, 2018.

Tilborgh, Louis van, and Ella Hendriks. "The Tokyo *Sunflowers*: A Genuine Repetition by Van Gogh or a Schuffenecker Forgery?" *Van Gogh Museum Journal*, 2001, pp. 16–43. https://www.dbnl.org/tekst/_van012200101_01/_van012200101_01_0003.php.

Uhlenbeck, Chris, Louis van Tilborgh, and Shigeru Oikawa. *Japanese Prints: The Collection of Vincent van Gogh*. Thames & Hudson, 2018.

Veldhorst, Natascha. *Van Gogh and Music: A Symphony in Blue and Yellow*. Translated by Diane Webb. Yale University Press, 2018.

Vellekoop, Marije, Muriel Geldof, Ella Hendriks, Leo Jansen, and Alberto de Tagle, eds. *Van Gogh's Studio Practice*. Van Gogh Museum, 2013.

Ward, Martha. "Impressionist Installations and Private Exhibitions." *Art Bulletin* 73, no. 4 (December 1991): 599–622. https://doi.org/10.2307/3045832.

Westheider, Ortrud, and Michael Philipp, eds. *Van Gogh: Still Lifes*. Exh. cat., Museum Barberini, Potsdam. Prestel, 2019.

Zemel, Carol M. *Van Gogh's Progress: Utopia, Modernity, and Late-Nineteenth-Century Art*. California Studies in the History of Art 36. University of California Press, 1997.

Acknowledgments

Vincent van Gogh wrote to the art critic Albert Aurier on February 9 or 10, 1890, that his *Sunflowers* "express an idea symbolizing 'gratitude.'" It is fitting, then, that a book on his paintings of these flowers ends with an expression of gratitude for the many individuals who made possible this publication and the exhibition it accompanies, *Van Gogh's Sunflowers: A Symphony in Blue and Yellow.*

Our appreciation goes first and foremost to our colleagues at the National Gallery, London, whose extraordinary partnership has presented Philadelphia audiences with the rare opportunity of seeing two *Sunflowers* side by side. For their collegiality and support we thank Sir Gabriele Finaldi, Chiara Di Stefano, Neil Evans, Grace Hailstone, Sarah Herring, Tracy Jones, Christopher Riopelle, Samantha Saward, and Susan Thompson. Significant recent scholarship on the *Sunflowers* in the collections of the National Gallery and the Van Gogh Museum in Amsterdam encouraged us to embark on a new study of our own painting. The examination of the Philadelphia *Sunflowers* was guided in our Conservation department by Teresa Lignelli, whose curiosity and attentive eye helped us to better understand the uniquely unvarnished and textured surface of the picture. Jason Wierzbicki's X-radiograph, infrared reflectography, and raking-light images revealed less observable aspects of the composition. Museum scientists Kate Duffy and Aleksandra Popowich identified traces of charcoal drawing on the primed canvas and investigated the presence of bromine containing eosin dye, indicative of a geranium lake pigment. The materials Van Gogh used were explored using X-ray fluorescence equipment at the nearby Barnes Foundation. We thank our Barnes colleagues Barbara Buckley and Anya Shutov for their collaboration and insight.

The exhibition at the Philadelphia Museum of Art reflects the work of many hands. From installing art to sweeping floors, from editing and typesetting labels to directing visitors through the building, from managing art shipments to ensuring stable and secure gallery conditions, a vast professional team is necessary to the realization of every exhibition. For their dedicated work on this project, I am grateful to Paul Brinkley, James Coyne, Michael Gibbons, Eric Griffin, Chris Havlish, Tim Jackson, Rebecca Kolodziejczak, Paul Koneazny, Eric McDade, Zachary McKinney, Tessa Paul, Hiro Sakaguchi, and Joseph Troiani in Installation and Packing; Christopher Ferguson in Conservation; Wynne Kettell, Danielle McAdams, and Morgan Webb in Registration; Kathryn Babbs Miller, Yana Balson, and Shayna Brodnick in Special Exhibitions; Rebecca Murphy in European Art; and Andrew Slavinskas in Exhibition Design. The interpretative materials and accompanying Bloomberg Connects audio tour were made in partnership with Rosalie Hooper and Dakota Stevens in Interpretation; Luis Bravo, Tammi Coxe, Gretchen Dykstra, James Paris, Erika Remmy, and Sarah Roche in Editorial and Graphic Design produced the compelling graphics. Stephen Keever in Information and Interpretive Technologies provided important technical assistance. The Facilities and Operations and Protection Services staff keep everything running at the museum, and Jeanine Clothier, Jonathan Cooper, Warren Duane, Deric Johnson, and Adrian Wiggins have been valued partners on this project, along with every security officer. In Curatorial Affairs, Sumner Bridenbaugh, Leslie Essoglou, Nhi Le, Louis Marchesano, and Jessica Todd Smith helped to guide the exhibition in partnership with the Executive Office and Daniel H. Weiss, who has supported the project since becoming director in December 2025. The Communications and Marketing teams of Courtney Anderson, Marcia Birbilis, Laura Coogan, Josie Hall, Sara Hernon-Reeves, and Jordan Tucker spread word of the exhibition to audiences in Philadelphia and beyond. Inside the museum, staff ensure its success daily by welcoming every visitor; my thanks go to Joshua Frank and the entire Visitor Services team for their nimble management of crowds. Dan Miller and the museum's dedicated volunteer guides are faithful partners in interpreting and sharing the collection with visitors.

Finding something new to say about Van Gogh's *Sunflowers*, some of the most recognizable and beloved still lifes in the world, is daunting. I am grateful to my colleagues Tara Contractor at the Philadelphia Museum of Art and Caroline Shields at the Art Gallery of Ontario, Toronto, for joining me in situating the *Sunflowers* within Van Gogh's time in Arles and Saint-Rémy-de-Provence, and within his conversations with Paul Gauguin and his ambitions for the presentation and display of his art. Our research was aided by Natalie Koziar, Bree Midavaine, and Rylyn Monahan in the Library and Archives. Jeffrey Werner diligently researched and secured photography and image rights, and Sarah Croop, with Aimee Almstead, provided additional photography support. The editing of the volume was overseen with meticulous care by Sarah Noreika, with whom it was a pleasure to work once again. Myriad details relating to the book and its production were overseen by Kathleen Krattenmaker and Richard Bonk, whose gracious support and encouragement are warmly appreciated. For the publication's thoughtful design we owe thanks to Sabine Hahn, whose eye for color, attention to detail, and appreciation of Van Gogh's painted surfaces have made the book in your hands the next best thing to being in front of the canvases.

—*Jennifer A. Thompson*
March 2026

Published on the occasion of the exhibition
Van Gogh's Sunflowers: A Symphony in Blue and Yellow
Philadelphia Museum of Art, June 6–October 11, 2026

Van Gogh's Sunflowers: A Symphony in Blue and Yellow was made possible by the Gloria and Jack Drosdick Fund for Special Exhibitions and the Harriet and Ronald Lassin Fund for Special Exhibitions.

All exhibitions at the Philadelphia Museum of Art are underwritten by the Annual Exhibition Fund. Generous support is provided by Andrea Baldeck, M.D.; Julia and David Fleischner; Robert Hayes; and Mark W. Strong and Dana Strong.

Credits as of February 13, 2026

Produced by the Publishing Department
Philadelphia Museum of Art
Kathleen Krattenmaker
The William T. Ranney Director of Publishing
2525 Pennsylvania Avenue
Philadelphia, PA 19130-2440
philamuseum.org

Distributed by Yale University Press
302 Temple Street
P.O. Box 209040
New Haven, CT 06520-9040
yalebooks.com/art

Edited by Sarah Noreika
Production by Richard Bonk
Designed by Sabine Hahn Grafik, Berlin
Proofread by Dianne Woo
Printed in Spain by Brizzolis, arte en gráficas

Details and Quotations
Front cover and flap: Vincent van Gogh, *Sunflowers*, January 1889 (see pp. 22–23); back cover and flap: Vincent van Gogh, *Sunflowers*, August 1888 (see pp. 10–11); pp. 2–3: Vincent van Gogh to Theo van Gogh, Arles, August 21 or 22, 1888, letter 666; pp. 40–41: Vincent van Gogh, *Sunflowers*, January 1889 (see pp. 22–23); pp. 60–61: Vincent van Gogh, *Sunflowers*, August 1888 (see pp. 10–11); pp. 94–95: Vincent van Gogh, *Sunflowers*, January 1889 (see pp. 26–27); pp. 98–99: Vincent van Gogh to Paul Gauguin, Arles, January 21, 1889, letter 739

Photographs were supplied by the owners and/or the following: The Barnes Foundation, Philadelphia: fig. 29; Basil & Elise Goulandris Foundation, Athens: fig. 28 (photograph by Chris Doulgeris); Bayerische Staatsgemäldesammlungen, Neue Pinakothek, Munich: p. 15; The Israel Museum, Jerusalem: fig. 22 (photograph by Ofrit Rosenberg); Kröller-Müller Museum, Otterlo, Netherlands: fig. 36 (photograph by Rik Klein Gotink); The Metropolitan Museum of Art, New York / Art Resource, NY: figs. 1, 3, 9, 11 (photograph by Malcolm Varon), 16; Musée des Beaux-Arts d'Orléans: fig. 14; Musée d'Orsay, Paris, RMN-Grand Palais / Art Resource, NY: figs. 6 (photograph by Hervé Lewandowski), 26 (photograph by Sophie Crépy); The Museum of Modern Art, New York / Art Resource, NY, licensed by SCALA: fig. 15; The National Gallery, London: p. 11, fig. 17; National Gallery of Art, Washington, DC: figs. 10, 24; Philadelphia Museum of Art Photo Studio: p. 23, figs. 2, 4, 20, 31, 38; Sompo Museum of Art, Tokyo: p. 19; Van Gogh Museum, Amsterdam: p. 27, figs. 5, 7, 8, 12, 13, 18, 19, 21, 27, 33, 34a,b, 35; The Wildenstein Plattner Institute: fig. 25

Library of Congress Control Number: 2026931172

Authorized Representative in the EU:
Easy Access System Europe
Mustamäe tee 50
10621 Tallinn, Estonia
gpsr.requests@easproject.com

ISBN: 978-0-87633-312-9

10 9 8 7 6 5 4 3 2 1